W I L L I A

Questions
That
Make The Sale

DARTNELL

4660 Ravenswood Avenue
Chicago, IL 60640
Phone: 800.621.5463
800.441.7878 (In Canada)

DARTNELL is a publisher serving the world of business with books, manuals, newsletters and bulletins, and training materials for executives, managers, supervisors, salespeople, financial officials, personnel executives, and office employees. Dartnell also produces management and sales training videos and audiocassettes, publishes many useful business forms, and many of its materials and films are available in languages other than English. Dartnell, established in 1917, serves the world's business community. For details, catalogs, and product information, write to:

THE DARTNELL CORPORATION,
4660 N Ravenswood Ave,
Chicago, IL 60640-4595, U.S.A.
or phone (800) 621-5463, in U.S. and Canada.

Dartnell Training Limited
125 High Holborn
London, England
WC1V 6QA
or phone 011-44-071-404-1585

This publication is designed to provide accurate and authoritative information in regard to the subject matter covered. It is sold with the understanding that the publisher is not engaged in rendering legal, accounting, or other professional service. If legal advice or other expert assistance is required, the services of a competent professional person should be sought.

From a Declaration of Principles jointly adopted by a Committee of the American Bar Association and a Committee of Publishers.

Published by The Dartnell Corporation
4660 N Ravenswood Ave
Chicago, IL 60640-4595
Chicago/Boston/London

©1992 The Dartnell Corporation

ISBN 0-85013-196-0

Printed in the U.S.A. by the Dartnell Corporation
1098765432

Dedication

To my Mother,
Who wondered if I would ever
stop asking questions
and
To my wife Sheila,
who knows that I won't.

Acknowledgments

There have been many people who have helped me with this book during the one year of writing and the 40 years of gathering material. I would like to thank them all.

I would especially like to acknowledge Eleanor Dugan for her expertise and care in editing my rough manuscript and to Rich Hagle, my editor at Dartnell. Also special thanks goes to Dorothy Nelson for her patience and her organization and to Zan Sloan for her typing and suggestions on the first draft.

Most important is my thanks to my wife and business partner, Sheila, for all her support, her encouragement and her understanding. It would never have been written without her . . .

Table of Contents

Table of Contents (Cont'd)

Preface

Why This Book?

Someone said to me, "You're so great at always asking the right questions. Where did you learn to do that?" I answered, "I learned it from experience." "And where," he asked, "did you get your experience?" My answer: "From asking the wrong questions."

In this book I'm going to share the insights and knowledge I've gained from more than thirty years of sales experience, and hopefully spare you a few of the crushing encounters that all salespeople face. I know which questions are almost guaranteed to make a sale and which will earn a fast "no." The reason I know the difference between "right" and "wrong" questions is that I have asked plenty of both kinds. That's why I'm eager to save you some of the bruises I experienced.

But even after you've read this book carefully, you are still going to ask a question now and then that doesn't get the answer you're looking for. That's how you get the experience that makes you an even better questioner.

How Has Selling Changed?

Remember the salesman character on the TV program *WKRP in Cincinnati*, Herb Tarlick? He was a sharp dresser—plaid polyester jacket, white belt and white shoes. Herb was a caricature of the old-time wheeling-dealing salesmen. We laughed at his antics because the days of the flashily-dressed, fast-talking, hard-hitting, oily-tongued, less-than-scrupulous extrovert salesperson have pretty much passed. Selling today requires different skills and a very different attitude. The complexity of our economy, advances in technology, and the need for service-oriented sales all demand a new type of salesperson.

Selling in the 1990s must be recognized as a profession. Years ago, barbers were usually surgeons and mechanics were engineers. Even a few years back salespeople were often thought of as flimflam artists. But the skills needed for surgeons, engineers, and salespeople have changed, and our perceptions have changed with them. Selling is a profession when it matches the buyer to the supplier and successfully fulfills both their needs.

The sales profession is an indispensable part of our complex and fragile economic ecosystem. This is not an exaggeration: the salespeople of the 1990s will play an enormous role in our nation's economic survival. They will challenge the traditional selling techniques that have worked well for decades because our world has changed. In traditional selling, the salesperson's function was to create the sale. Today's selling is different because:

- *Buyers are different.* They are more educated and sophisticated in their choices because of the media—television, radio and print. Often they are presold on a product through advertising and publicity before the salesperson comes on the scene.

- *Regulations are different.* Laws, licensing, and consumer protection statutes and practices limit the exuberance of the traditional salesperson. "Caveat emptor" (let the buyer beware) is backed up by government regulations, such as the three-day "right to cancel" clause.

- *Buying procedures are different.* It used to be that the purchasing agent had the major decision-making power. Now purchasing committees headed by assistant vice presidents or district managers decide jointly. Often their decisions must then be okayed by someone else even higher up. These compartmentalized institutional decisions can make selling as indirect a form of communication as tossing note-filled bottles into the ocean.

- *Presentations are different.* Today salespeople are asked to present product data directly to the prospect's computer for price analysis. Much selling is done via prepackaged audiovisual presentations with the salesperson, if there is one, acting as M.C. Often fax communication has replaced the face-to-face kind.
- *Promotion is different.* Rather than putting money into a network of well-trained salespeople who are backed up by advertising, some companies are concentrating on advertising alone to presell their product or service.
- *Packaging is different.* Products are now designed to sit all alone on shelves and sell themselves through attractive labels and comprehensive instructions. Customers pick a product and take their selections to a check-out stand where a cashier is ready to take their money. The "selling" is not done by a live salesperson.

Are Basics Obsolete?

In spite of these changes, traditional selling techniques still constitute the bottom-line basics of selling in this decade. However, not all salespeople of the old school have discovered how to adapt these techniques to today's buying environment. In frustration, they either quit or abandon what they know and simply go around collecting purchase agreements for their company's presold products.

Even worse, many new salespeople are little more than glorified order takers. Some rely so much on preselling that they never learn sales basics. For them selling involves no individual or personal effort. They are choosing the safety and comfort of calling on prospects that are presold by some form of advertising but losing the thrill of selling by using their personal creativity.

So what do today's salespeople do to avoid being just order takers. Here are some basic techniques.

First Basic: Know Your Product

The first sales basic for the professional salesperson is product knowledge. When was the last time you asked a question about a product or service and waited while the salesperson looked up the answer? Were you told to call someone else who might know? Did you ever find out? If salespeople don't know more about what they're selling and what you need, then you don't need them! Nearly every individual is capable of researching, planning, choosing, and solving his or her own needs. Professional salespeople know it's their job to save prospects this time and effort.

Second Basic: Service

The second basic for today's professional is understanding the power and importance of real customer service. Our office got a phone call that perfectly illustrates the modern "order taker" mentality. We recently purchased a new copy machine. A young man called to let us know that we could get a big price break on toner if we ordered within three days. "Do you want to place an order?" I heard our secretary asking him about a problem we were having with the machine. It became obvious she wasn't getting any help so I came on line. The young man said that he knew nothing about how the copiers worked. He just sold toner. We would have to call the service department.

I asked him if he could transfer the call. "No, we're not at the same number." Could he give us the number? "No, I don't have it," he replied, "but I'm sure it must be in the phone book." By this time a potentially positive encounter had turned into a disaster.

He was a nice-sounding young man, but no one had ever taught him how to give service. Perhaps he was being clocked for how quickly he could take orders and get off the phone, as some phone solicitation companies do. Certainly he had no motivation to report our problem and to follow up on it. His company lost a lot of good will and future loyalty.

Third Basic: Selling Techniques

The third basic is knowing, understanding and using selling techniques. While some organizations offer their salespeople training in product knowledge and perhaps even in customer service, they often overlook training in basic sales techniques like qualifying, closing, or handling objections. Even professions that require extensive education before licensing—such as real estate, insurance, or financial planning—don't require any basic sales skills to obtain a license. To be successful in the 1990s, salespeople need to make a concentrated, continuing effort to learn, master, and apply selling techniques.

Selling is a game of fundamentals, much like golf. You must learn the techniques and then practice them over and over until you approach perfection.

What are the basic techniques of selling? They are:

- prospecting
- qualifying
- building rapport
- making the presentation
- overcoming objections
- using trial closes
- closing the sale
- follow-up

For the field salesperson, add:

- getting the appointment
- getting referrals

All these basic selling techniques use the most important basic skill of all: *knowing how to ask questions.*

So, despite a change in style, today's salesperson will benefit greatly from learning the basics of selling—especially that most basic technique, the art of asking questions. This book is going to show you how to ask questions, when to ask, where to ask, and what to ask. Does that sound like a good idea?

Non-Manipulative Selling?

You may have heard and read about the new "non-manipu-lative selling." Honestly, there is no such thing. *Manipulating* is a much-abused word. After all, paints are manipulated into great paintings, words are manipulated into books, and cook-ing ingredients into gourmet cuisine. Manipulating doesn't have to mean exploiting someone or being unscrupulous. If you can substitute words like *moving, directing, controlling, organizing,* and *forming* for the kind of manipulating that you do, then you're an ethical, modern selling pro.

Of course, today's salesperson can no longer regard sell-ing as conquering, see a sale as a battle won, or consider customers as so many scalps on the belt. Fortunately this kind of manipulating, the age-old stereotype of selling as coercion and flimflam, has faded.

Nevertheless, selling is still manipulating, no matter how you look at it. As a salesperson, your job is to discover the prospects' needs and wants through questioning and more questioning, and then to show the prospect how many of those needs and wants can be fulfilled by your product or service.

Should modern salespeople be honest? Yes, scrupulously so! But that doesn't mean that you must point out all the reasons the prospect shouldn't buy, unless it's to illustrate how the pluses outweigh the minuses. People would rarely do *anything* if they considered only the negatives. Profes-sional salespeople still focus on the positive benefits of their product or service and soft-pedal the unfavorable points.

Real service is the basis of today's selling. The profession-als want to serve and firmly believe what they are selling will benefit the customer. They ask questions to discover or con-firm the customer's needs and wants so they can serve them better. If they don't believe they can serve, they excuse them-selves to get on to the next prospect.

Yes, as a skilled questioner you will learn how to "manip-ulate" your prospects positively. Yes, skilled questioning will help you identify and satisfy your clients' real needs. Yes, questions will help you close the sale. To do any less is to be an order taker, not a salesperson. Some people may choose to think of this fact-finding selling process as manipulation. I choose to call it service!

We are told this is the service age. More than half the workers in the United States now work in service industries, yet the overwhelming complaint of consumers is poor service. How better to serve your customers than by *asking* to fill their needs?

1

Why Questions?

"What would you like to have before your dessert today?"
Sells out homemade desserts every lunchtime at a neighborhood diner. (See page 2.)

"Who wants to go jump in the lake?"
Retrieved and sold jewelry that had just fallen overboard. (See page 17.)

"Could you help me out with a little change?"
Earned $40,000 a year, part time and tax free. (See page 18.)

Why questions? Because, if you want to be a professional salesperson, asking questions is the only way to sell. Selling isn't telling, it's *asking*. When you learn what to ask and how to ask it, you are suddenly able to do two powerful and seemingly contradictory things:

1. You take control of the selling situation. That's because the power of questions is in the asking, not the answering.
2. You change your customers' perception of you from a possible adversary to trusted adviser. Professionals know that it's no longer possible to win a sale by challenging customers, by overcoming their resistance or by "defeating" them. With questions you become their valuable ally and expert consultant. You no longer do things *to* or *for* your prospects, but *with* them.

When you understand the art of questioning, you achieve extraordinary results. Knowing when, where, and how to ask can:

- Capture and keep the prospect's attention.
- Reveal the prospect's motivations for buying (or not buying).
- "Qualify" your prospects, check their boundaries of comfort, and identify their interests.
- Focus your prospects on the issues you want them to consider.
- Prove to your prospects that you really care about them and their problems.
- Indicate when your prospects are ready to buy.

"Questions," says master seminar organizer John Hammond, "give salespeople a barometer to find out if they are on track with the sales process." Allison Wilson of CNN agrees on the importance of questions: "It's not what you say, it's what you ask. If you do too much talking at first and don't ask questions, it's like 'spilling your candy in the lobby' before the show begins."

Asking the Right Questions

If you love dessert, don't arrive late for lunch at Nini's Coffee Shop in San Mateo, California. Rick Swartz, the owner, has developed a question technique for his staff that sells all their homemade desserts long before the end of each lunch period. The other day I observed my waitress, Michon Mahlstedt in action. She approached each new customer with her order pad out and asked, *"What would you like to have before your dessert today?"*

All the customers laughed. Most ordered or asked about the special. But if they said "Gee, I don't know" or "I'm not having any dessert," she would ask, "Don't you want to consider our delicious homemade amaretto cake with low-cal whipped cream?" On another day I watched her coworker

Denise Clohessy, sell an entire eight-slice pie in less than five minutes. She asked the right questions.

As you go through this book, you'll probably be surprised at how easily the right questions can influence people and how easy these questions are to ask. You'll learn the kinds of questions that work best in each of the progressive stages of the sale—prospecting, qualifying, probing, presenting, closing, and the post-sale follow-up. You'll also learn the one question you should probably never ask.

How, When, and Where to Ask Questions

That's easy. Ask in person. Ask on the phone. Ask by letter. Ask by FAX. However you do it, ASK, ASK, ASK!

Never be embarrassed to say, "Can you help me?" No one can succeed in selling who doesn't learn to ask. When you ask people to tell you something or to do something, you bring them actively into the selling situation. You also give them an incredible gift: you make them feel important because *they* can help you!

Warning: Don't get carried away. Don't use the power of questioning aggressively. That means no cross-examinations, no third degree. Never demand. Pressure creates tension. So ask for what you want, even asking if it's okay to ask. My friend John Hammond says, "A lot of salespeople overlook something important in the information gathering stage. They need to get permission to ask questions:

> *'Mr. Bethel, we've been able to help thousands of people here at the XYZ company. We may be able to help you—I don't know if we can or not—but to determine that, may I ask you a few questions? You don't mind if I ask you a few questions, do you?'*

"If you don't ask permission," says John, "you risk two situations. Either the prospects may be reluctant to answer a lot of questions because they're not sure what's in it for them—or else you'll find yourself hesitating to ask the questions you need to ask."

Even if you get permission to ask a specific number of questions—two, say, or three—each question can expand into sub-questions according to the prospect's responses. Ask with a pleasant, confident attitude of someone who expects cooperation. That's how you get what you want.

Meeting Resistance

What if you meet with resistance? In my seminars I demonstrate how the salesperson's attitude can create resistance like this: I approach someone in the audience and say in a firm voice, "Put out your hand." The subjects usually look puzzled, uneasy, hesitant, but after all they've come to learn so they extend their hands. I then place my palm against theirs and push. Invariably they push back—they resist. We both push harder until it becomes a power struggle. That's creating resistance. Then I walk up to another person, extend my hand and ask congenially, "May I shake your hand?" The person smiles and we shake hands. No resistance. Asking in a friendly manner helps to build mutual trust. If you show concern and care, you usually get cooperation.

You can never lose by asking as long as you are willing to give in return. Asking is a can't lose proposition. If you ask and someone says "no," you are no worse off than you were before you asked. But if you ask, and someone says "yes," you win!

The Five Kinds of Questions

There are five major categories of questions. Let's cover them now so you'll recognize them as we work through the stages of the sale:

- Open-end questions
- Reflective questions
- Directive questions

- Multiple-choice questions
- Closed-end questions

Open-end questions can't be answered with a yes or no response. Their strength is that they solicit information about emotions and thoughts. Open-end questions are used to gather information. You design them to find out what is really on the prospect's mind while you introduce your own ideas. The open-end question relies on the classic "Five W's and an H" of journalism—Who, What, Where, When, Why and sometimes How.

Some open-end questions are:

- What do you think?
- Where could this be improved?
- When would that make a difference?
- How would you react if ...?

Open-end questions reveal opinions and feelings along with facts. "Why's" are a particularly good way to attempt to close a sale when things are not going your way. Ask "Why?" with surprise in your voice. This will probably get you the real reason for the objection, or it will force them to clarify their previously-stated objections, or it may cause them to waver and reconsider. If they respond with a strong objection, you'll know what you have to deal with.

"Why?" has always worked well for me, but there is one top salesman, Rich Goldman, who swears he never uses it. Rich is senior vice president and general sales manager for Television Program Enterprises, a division of Cox Broadcasting. He told me why he avoids "Why?":

> If a prospect says, "I don't agree that your product would suit me or benefit me," your gut reaction is usually "why?" That's a word that I've tried not to use because it challenges the prospect's beliefs. There's a way to ask why without asking why: "Evidently you've got a reason for feeling that way? Would you be

*willing to tell me what it is?" Generally they do
and you learn their true feelings.
     For example, if they say: "Well, yes . . .
you're too expensive," then you can ask, "If we
assume for the moment that dollars are not a
consideration, then you would be interested?"
Then if they say, "Well, no," you have narrowed down the objection. "Obviously there's
something else then that is troubling you?"*

A *reflective question* takes a previous question or statement
and turns it into another question by rephrasing it. Reflective
questions give the prospect an opportunity to rethink, review,
or restate the thoughts and ideas that led to the previous
answer. They help you determine the true objections or problems while fixing favorable reactions in the prospect's mind.
Some reflective questions are:

- Then you feel that your situation is . . . ?
- John, you believe this method would . . . ?
- You tried something like this, Mary, and you feel . . . ?
- As of now your experience has shown . . . ?
- Let's see if I'm clear about this. You're saying that . . . ?

Reflective questions help you clarify and define areas of
concern that your prospect may not be aware of or has not be
able to express. When using reflective questions, keep genuine concern in your tone of voice and keep any judgmental
tone out. Remember, people don't care how much you know
until they know how much you care.

Directive questions focus the prospect on the decision you
want them to make. They are often used in trial closings.
That's when you take the sales temperature to see if the
prospect is ready to buy. Your question expands a given idea
or a given point, or you clarify the prospect's thoughts, or
your question helps the prospect decide that the overall benefits are desirable. The words "would," "could," and "should"

are helpful in asking a directive question. Some directive questions are:

- Mr. Jones, how much money/time do you think this benefit would save you?
- Kate, where do you feel you could gain the most if. . . .
- In what ways would this plan be better than your old one, Bob?
- So you agree, Mrs. Stone, that this service would/could/should. . . .

Directive questions expand on an idea, clarify a thought or help the prospect understand a benefit.

Multiple-choice questions are a form of directive questions. They can be used to move the prospect along the path to the sale. We all love being offered choices. Choice is what a free market economy is about, but choices can be directed. Every smart parent knows that you never ask children if they want to wear a coat. Instead you ask, "Do you want to wear your red sweater or your blue jacket to the park?"

Multiple-choice questions can direct attention to the decisions that make up the sale:

- Would you like delivery on Tuesday or Wednesday?
- Red or black?
- Cash or charge?
- Regular size or the large economy size?
- Would you like to buy one more and get a 15% discount for bulk buying?
- Tinted glass? Wire wheels? Stereo or radio? Leather seats? Sunroof? Stick shift?

Don't overdo choices. Recently I walked into a coffee shop, hungry for breakfast.

Waiter: What would you like this morning?
Me: Eggs, bacon, potatoes, and coffee.
Waiter: How would you like your eggs? Fried or scrambled? Do you want the bacon crisp or extra crisp?

> Would you like the potatoes plain or with onions and pepper? Would you like toast with that? White, wheat, rye, raisin toast, or an English muffin? What kind of jam? Strawberry, grape, or marmalade? Regular or decaffeinated coffee? Black or with cream?

I started to lose my appetite. Choice is great, but too many choices can be overwhelming. Professionals know when to stop.

Closed-end questions require a "yes" or "no" answer or a simple fact: "Do you rent or own your office building?" Closed-end questions are useful for narrowing down options quickly. That can be good or bad. Novice salespeople, to their sorrow, tend to overuse closed-end questions. When you ask a question that requires a yes/no answer, you may be betting on a "yes." If the prospect says "no," your interview could be over. However, if you need to know whether you are talking to an actual prospect or you are ready to try to close the sale, you may decide to use a closed-end question.

Inexperienced salespeople often back themselves into corners with closed-end questions. They use them prematurely in a trial close by asking:

Q: "Do you understand what I mean?"
A: "Nope." (Then the salesperson must start over.)
Q: "Is this a product you'd like to buy?"
A: "Nope." (Then the salesperson has lost the sale.)

Just before asking for the sale, you can try a preclosing closed-end question. These help you confirm that the prospect is ready to buy. (Note how a "no" answer can sometimes mean "yes" to the sale.)

- Can you think of any reasons why this wouldn't work for you?
- Have we covered all your concerns?

- Have I shown you how this is going to pay for itself in six months?
- Is there any other product/service that you know of that can beat ours?

All the above closed-end questions either close the sale or give you an opportunity to continue. There is a classic George Burns and Gracie Allen comedy routine that illustrates how to benefit from "no" for an answer.

George:	Gracie, I want you to learn how to say "no" to salesmen. Whatever they say, you answer "no!" Let's hear you say it.
Gracie:	No!
George:	The next time a salesman comes to the door, that's the only word I want you to say.

* * *

Salesperson:	Good day, Madame. Do you have a yacht?
Gracie:	No!
Salesperson:	Would one be too expensive for you?
Gracie:	No!
Salesperson:	Do you think your husband would object if you bought one?
Gracie:	No!
Salesperson:	Splendid, I see you're both boating enthusiasts. Would one yacht be enough?
Gracie:	No!
Salesperson:	Ah, you'll take one for each of you. Will tomorrow be soon enough for delivery?
Gracie:	No!
Salesperson:	This afternoon, then. Would you like easy credit terms?
Gracie:	No!
Salesperson:	That'll be C.O.D. $100,000.

Closed-end questions can be dangerous, but don't avoid them completely. Use them sparingly or when you feel certain the prospect is ready to make a decision.

Answering Questions with Questions

Your prospects will have a lot of questions of their own, questions they ask to decide whether what you're offering is right for them. You'll answer all their questions, of course, but, whenever possible, retain control by answering each question with another question. When the ancient Greek philosopher Socrates was asked how he was doing, he replied "Compared to what?"

By using "throw-back" questions—questioning the question—your prospects must continue to clarify their own thinking.

Q: Is this the best price you can give us?
A: Is 10% above wholesale low enough?

Q: Will you be there between 5:00 and 6:00?
A: Do you want to make an appointment for then?

Q: Is this really unbreakable?
A: What if I agree to replace it free if it ever breaks?

To answer your questions, prospects must think through their position and then explain or defend it. Professionals rarely defend their position. *Do* explain, *do* provide additional information, but, whenever it's possible, let the prospect provide the reasons why this information is meaningful.

Of course you'll supply facts and figures when requested, but you can piggyback them on throw-back questions:

- This truck gets 45 miles to the gallon with a ten-ton load. How does that compare with your current average? Oh, you've never computed what it costs you per ton/mile? Shall we stop to figure that?
- The total price is $998 per unit plus a $25 installation fee. Would you want us to install them, or do you prefer doing that yourself?
- We have several payment plans. Would you like to go over them now?

My dear friend, Ernie Gonzalez, is a master at throw-back questions. If someone asks, "Does it come in red?" Ernie replies, "Is that the color that would help you make a favorable decision? Do you really want it in red?" He poses throwback questions until he leads the prospect to define and decide exactly what is necessary to say yes. Ernie makes prospects take a position and defend it. If he had stated his position, the prospect might have doubted or challenged it. But when prospects reach their own decision through the questioning process, it is *theirs* and they are committed to defending it.

So, why do salespeople often answer a question with a question? Can you suggest a better way?

Irish Questions

I'm half Irish so I can tell one of my favorite Irish stories. A young Irish actor got his first Broadway role, a walk-on with one line: "It is." He rehearsed it over and over, giving it every inflection he could think of. On opening night, he strode confidently on stage, turned to the leading lady, and said "Isn't it?"

The Irish are famous (or is it infamous?) for ending every statement with a question mark:

- Nice day, isn't it?
- It will be dark soon, won't it?
- You're American, aren't you?

Professional salespeople know that they can get a prospect's attention and confirmation just by adding a question at the end of each statement:

- This service will save you time, don't you agree?
- Your secretary could use this, couldn't she?
- You're coming to the demonstration, aren't you?
- This product will solve that problem, won't it?
- This would look great in your office, wouldn't it?

If they disagree, you have the salesperson's second most valuable asset, an objection. (See Chapter 7 on objections.) If they agree, you have a confirmation. If you get enough confirmations during your interaction, you can assume the sale.

One salesman I was training told me: "I'm not very good at getting confirmations, am I?" But he was, wasn't he? He asked a question at the end of his statement, and that's how you get a confirmation, isn't it?

Keep Questions Short and Simple

Ask one question at a time and don't make it too long. Listeners confuse easily. Novice questioners may bombard prospects with multiple part questions: "Well, have you thought over what we discussed last week and have you changed your mind and what would happen now if we...." The stunned prospect doesn't know which question to respond to first and starts to drown in "self-talk" about possible answers. The result is "Uhh..." followed by silence.

When you have a list of questions you want to ask, use them one at a time. Pose the question, then keep absolutely quiet so you can really hear the *entire* answer. When the prospect stops talking, pause to be sure they have finished. Look for body language to indicate whether the prospect is still mulling over the question. If a look or gesture clearly indicates the ball is back in your court, don't automatically go on to the next question on your list. Show that you've really listened by making your second question responsive to their answer. This is where professional salespeople learn to excel.

If "thinking on your feet" comes hard for you at first, you could work out a chart of every possible answer to question #1. Under each answer, list the appropriate question #2, and under it every possible answer. Under each of those answers, list a good question #3. You'll wind up with a giant tree, like an inverted genealogy chart. Study it and have someone quiz you occasionally until you feel comfortable tailoring your question sequence to a wide variety of problems and concerns. But don't count on memorization to replace *listening and responding!*

Listen to the Answers

Just asking isn't enough. Ask. Listen. Ask again. Then restate the prospect's answers to be sure that you understand. When you do this, you help people to confront their own fuzzy thinking, prejudices, or incomplete understanding of the relevant issues.

Good listening frees the prospects to tell you their stories. Listen to their *feelings*, not just their words. Make them know that you really care. One of the greatest salesmen who ever worked for me was a fellow named Keith Sheffield. Keith had a very simple but powerful listening philosophy: "The customer is the most important thing in my life *right now.*" He was an amazing salesman because he convinced customers that they *were* the most important person in the world.

A study by Dr. Paul Rankin presented at an Ohio State Educational Conference showed that typical adults spend about 70 percent of their waking hours communicating with others. A follow-up doctoral study on listening by Dr. Lyman K. Steil confirmed Rankin's figures and broke the communication activity down into these proportions:

- writing   9 %
- reading   16 %
- talking   30 %
- listening 45 %

If you spend so much time listening, you ought to be darn good at it, right? Not necessarily. Some people hear but don't listen for full understanding. Hearing is passive. Listening is active and requires your full attention. Here are some common causes of ineffective listening:

- You may focus so intently on something the prospect has said that you miss what comes after and lose the main point. (In your trouble-shooting probing stage, people rarely describe problems in a logical order, starting with the most important point.)

- You may be thinking about the answer you will give as soon as the prospect stops talking.
- You may be distracted by something going on in the room, by your personal reaction to the prospect, by thoughts unrelated to the selling situation. ("If I don't finish up here in five minutes, my car is going to be towed.")

Regardless of the reason, when you don't listen completely, you miss selling opportunities.

Six Ways to Improve Your Listening Skills

1. Limit your own talking. You can't listen and talk at the same time.
2. Make the customers' problems and needs the most important thing in the world right here, right now. They are, aren't they?! You'll understand and retain information better.
3. Listen actively by asking questions about what has just been said. Give feedback. That means nodding once in a while, saying "Yes," "I understand," "You're saying that . . . ." Prove you're really listening. Clear up any points you don't understand immediately, but do it diplomatically.

Never say:

- I didn't understand.
- I don't follow you.
- I disagree.
- What you're trying to say is . . . .

Say instead:

- Let me see if I understand. Are you saying that . . . ?
- From what you've told me, the question seems to be . . . .
- That's certainly valid. Would another way to look at that be . . . ?

4. Don't interrupt. Sometimes a pause, even a long pause, doesn't mean that your prospect has exhausted a subject.
5. Concentrate on what the prospect is saying. Shut out outside distractions and your own internal "self-talk." Your prospect will know immediately if your mind is elsewhere.
6. Listen for *ideas*, not just the words being said. Try to identify the ideas that the customer is trying to put across. Take notes on key points. This will help you remember important points, while demonstrating your concern to the prospect.

Every good salesperson I've ever known has been an excellent listener. Maybe God was trying to tell us something when he gave us two ears and one mouth.

Eye-to-Eye

Be sure you look at prospects as you ask and listen—make strong eye contact. It makes people feel important and it keeps them focused on you. Can you imagine anything more disconcerting or insulting than to be talking with someone whose eyes constantly shift to look at something else in the room?

A saleswoman I knew, Ginny Morvey, once taught me the value of eye contact. She used it to get a good table in a crowded restaurant. Her secret was to make the maitre d' look her in the eye. Most of the time that isn't what happens. The maitre d' is looking down at his reservation list or across the room to spot a table. This lady wouldn't say a word to the maitre d' until he made eye contact. She had learned in her selling career that when you get people to look you in the eye, they treat you as a person, not an object. So keep eye contact as you listen to what your customer says.

There are some rare exceptions to the eye-contact rule. Our nation is so diverse and made up of people from so many backgrounds that it is important to be sensitive to ethnic

differences. In some cultures, staring someone straight in the
eye is regarded alternately as rude, seductive, disrespectful of
authority, or hostile. Western women can get into trouble
when they look directly at men from some eastern cultures—
such eye contact is reserved for prostitutes. In other societies,
a direct gaze may mean "step outside and repeat that, buddy."
So if you try to make eye contact and find the prospect
distinctly uncomfortable, look for clues that you are dealing
with a different cultural perception. Remember the true story
of the high school principal who expelled a student wrong-
fully accused of stealing: "I could tell she was lying when she
denied it because she wouldn't look me in the eye." However,
the girl came from a culture where proper young ladies never,
ever looked directly at people in authority.

So, put positive eye contact on your list of basic selling
skills while remembering that both eye contact and the com-
fort-zone of distance when two people hold a conversation
are subject to different cultural interpretations. Tune in to any
discomfort your prospect may be experiencing and adjust
your actions accordingly.

Use the Prospect's Name

Use the prospect's name frequently when asking questions.
People love to hear their own names. For example:

- Mr. Jones, what is your opinion about . . . ?
- What would happen, Ms. Stevens, if . . . ?
- Why is that important to you, Bob?

Using names adds power to your question because it keeps
the prospects' attention and makes them feel important.

- Bill, what do you think is a better way to . . . ?
- Where do you think we should start, Mr. Jones?
- What do *you* feel the real problem is, Mrs. Smith?

The more you mention the prospects' names, the better—
to a point. Don't get carried away and overdo it, or it will
seem phony and condescending.

"Who Knows How to Swim?"

The greatest question in sales is still any variation on "Maybe
you can help me?" People tend to help when someone asks.
Carol Kuhn used this human instinct to humorous advantage
when disaster struck one of her Lady Remington Fashion
Jewelry shows. Carol is an experienced hand at presenting
"home shows" in all sorts of settings. Once she was doing a
presentation for a group on a pontoon boat when a big wave
knocked some of her merchandise overboard. As everyone
watched in dismay, dozens of bright earrings and shiny neck-
laces, bracelets and pins sank slowly to the bottom of the
lake.

In a flash of inspiration, Carol cried: "Who wants to go
jump in the lake? An additional 50% discount on everything
you can retrieve!" The presentation party turned into a lively
and boisterous treasure hunt with non-swimmers cheering on
the divers. Now, technically, under maritime law, recovered
treasure is the property of the salvager, but every woman
insisted on paying for her baubles. Most of the pieces were
recovered and ordered on the spot.

Helping makes people feel important. We're taught from
childhood to help. When Mom asked you to help around the
house, you probably did. When your teacher asked you to
clean the erasers, you did. Today when you are asked to help
others, you give money or volunteer. Helping is a habit. I do
it. You do it.

But there is always a price to pay when you ask for help
and get it, a very low price, but an obligation nevertheless:

- You must show appreciation in return.
- You must show cooperation in return.
- You must give service in return.

When you ask for something, you are implying that you will do these three things. Always follow through on your unspoken contract.

The $40,000 Question

When I had my office in the financial district of San Francisco, I was often approached for a handout by a neat, middle-aged man in faded work clothes. He wasn't the usual panhandler. He was clean, neatly dressed, pleasant, and articulate. He politely asked everyone who passed: "Could you help me out with a little change?" Most people didn't stop, but a few did.

Month after month he stood there, and month after month my curiosity grew. Finally I stopped and asked him if I could buy five dollars of his time to ask him about his work. He agreed, for indeed he thought of what he was doing as a "job." He told me he worked five days a week, five hours a day: from 8:00 a.m. to 9:30 a.m., again during the lunch hour, and from 4:00 p.m. to 6:00 p.m. The most profitable hours were at lunch time. About one passerby in twenty gave him money, usually twenty-five or fifty cents, though every tenth "customer" gave him a dollar. His total earnings averaged $40,000 a year—tax free. He was very happy with his job: "Where else could I make this kind of money with no skills and no training, for just 30 hours a week?"

And why did people give him money? That's simple. Because he *asked* them to!

Learn to Ask

You can't spend too much time learning to ask. The Bible says, "Ask and you shall receive." Asking is the *only* way to receive. Professional salespeople get more information from their prospects than ordinary salespeople. Why? Because they ask.

In the following chapters you are going to learn how to ask the right questions in all phases of the selling process:

establishing motivation, prospecting, qualifying, probing, presenting, closing, and follow-up.

(Oh, yes, in case you were wondering, the one question you should probably never ask before you are ready to close is: "Would you like to buy this?")

_____

"If there is one single non-biological urge that all people have, it's to feel important. How can you do that? Ask your prospects questions and allow them to talk!"

Douglas E. Elwood
Sales Manager

_____

2

Motivation Questions

"Do you want to have fun?"
Sells more than $200,000 worth of trail bikes a year
in one tiny town. (See page 22.)

*"How would you feel if your kids got peanut
butter on your concert grand piano?"*
Sold *two* pianos. (See page 24.)

"Where do you want to put your couch?"
Sold 32 unbuilt condos in six weeks without a
demonstration model. (See page 29.)

How do you find people who want what you're selling? How do you even know where to start to look? You ask questions! Professional salespeople know that you have to find out why people *think* they are buying before you can pinpoint your prospects. Questions are the only way to uncover your prospects' needs, wants, hidden objectives, fears, prejudices, and doubts—their "buying motivations."

Some buying motivations seem straight-forward enough. Hungry people buy food. Carpenters buy wood and nails. But which food, which wood? Motivations are rarely simple. Decisions are influenced by cultural or environmental factors, by education, past experience, social status, income, and the opinions of friends, neighbors and family. All of these factors affect the strength of the buying motives and all vary from person to person and from time to time.

Every human being abounds with complex needs. The number and kind depend upon temperament, lifestyle, and cultural expectations. Some needs create tension which must be satisfied. This tension converts a need to a desire. Not until this stage is reached is the prospect ready to buy.

"Do You Want to Have Fun?"

Frank Snowden, a manufacturer's rep, told me how a few skillful questions about feelings made an unlikely dealer the nation's number one seller of trail bikes:

> When I first started selling Fisher Mountain Bikes, the second account we opened was in a tiny town called Pollock Pines, west of South Lake Tahoe, in the middle of nowhere. The town is basically a truck stop, and the weather there is often cold and nasty. Amazingly the dealer there, Gordon Bonser, turned out to be our best account.
>
> Gordon had a reputation as a good bike builder and avid cyclist. At first he sold only a few bikes a year, but he was very enthusiastic. When I went there to meet with him, I expected a rugged outdoor type. Instead I found a balding man about 5'3" and 275 pounds. I'm thinking, "How is this man ever going to sell a bike?" Then a customer came in.
>
> I watched Gordon sell a bike in less than twenty minutes without ever once mentioning the type of tubing, the type of rims, or the tires. He just asked a few questions about how the man felt about the outdoors, sunshine, exercise, and even picnics. Then he told the customer: "You're going to have a blast on this bike! You'll be outdoors in the sun. You can bring a picnic lunch with you . . . " Before I knew it, the customer

had bought the bike, a rack for the back, a basket for the picnic lunch, and Gordon had him out the door.

Gordon has been one of our #1 accounts nationally. These bikes cost between $1,000 and $2,500. He sells between 200 and 300 a year in this tiny town, and he has never sold one on the technical merits of the bike. Instead he sells fun. He always starts with a question. When other dealers tell me they can't do this, I ask, "What are you selling? Tubing and rims? Or *fun?*"

The Five Buying Motives

There are five basic buying motives. They work on both the positive and the negative emotions, the desire for gain and the fear of loss.

Surprisingly, people are usually more eager to prevent loss than they are to create gain. Think about it. Even though we all would enjoy winning, we sure as blazes don't want to *lose*.

Here are the five basic reasons that people buy:

1. *Profit.* People want gain, achievement, profit, a benefit of some sort.
2. *Peace of Mind.* Fear of loss is a major motivator. People want to protect what they have—their property, profits, health, loved ones, and future security. They want to save time and stop or avoid aggravation. They want a service that guards their interests. They want a product that will last and give good service—or, conversely, that can be easily discarded when it's no longer useful. All of these factors contribute to peace of mind.
3. *Pleasure.* Pleasure can be comfort, convenience, enjoyment, affection, admiration, luxury, or good health. Good health relates to all Five P's, but it is most positively linked

to pleasure. That's why advertisers say "it's fun to be healthy," rather than "you'll spend less on doctors." Pleasure includes an emphasis on youth, beauty, and sexual attraction. A glance at any form of advertising reveals an emphasis on appeals to pleasure in our society.

4. *Pain.* Most people want protection from pain—from extremes of heat and cold, from hunger, from illness, from stress, conflict, the complexities of life they'd rather not deal with, and even from plain old hard work.

5. *Pride.* This includes anything that lets someone say, "I am special." My partner and wife, Sheila Murray Bethel (author of *Making a Difference: 12 Qualities that Make You a Leader*), has coined the acronym PMMFI. It stands for: Please Make Me Feel Important.We all have an inborn need for approval, social acceptance, affection, admiration, and for feeling important. This is one of the most basic buyer motivations. There is a vast market for things that make us feel nurtured and cared about. People also experience pride when they perceive an advancement in their skills, lifestyle, attractiveness, power, control over themselves or others, or reputation. Luxury goods are often promoted in ways that appeal to this kind of pride. Pride may be one of the seven deadly sins, but it sells a lot of merchandise.

Which of the Five P's is your product or service most likely to appeal to: profit, peace of mind, pleasure, pain, or pride? Who is most likely to respond to each motivation? Will the motivations be constant factors for every potential buyer or will they vary from customer to customer? Can you design your approach so that your first question or two will reveal which of the Five P's are operating?

For example, the purchase of a fine piano is usually motivated by the desire for pleasure (playing it and listening) and pride ("This is a magnificent instrument"—"I'll sound like Rubinstein.") One piano salesperson I met knew how to ask questions that revealed a further buying motivation which, in turn, led to an even bigger sale.

My former wife was an accomplished pianist. One evening she and I went to the movies and found the line extending around the block. I persuaded her to go for a walk instead. We passed a piano store. An hour later—you guessed it—we had bought $9200 worth of pianos: a concert grand for her and an upright for the kids!

Here's how the salesperson did it. As he asked all the right questions to persuade her that now was the perfect time to acquire her dream piano, he was also asking casually about where we lived, our family, where she would put the piano, and who else would be playing it. Music, they agreed, was essential for enriching children's lives. Once the sale was closed for the concert grand, the salesperson asked innocently, "And how would you feel if your kids got peanut butter on your concert grand piano? What will happen when their friends come over and want to play it?"

Now, no musical parent is going to deny a child access to a piano, but the mental picture of young children running their toy trucks up and down that keyboard or getting peanut butter between the hand-carved keys of her Steinway was unendurable. It was logical therefore, even imperative to her peace of mind, that we have a *second* piano, an inexpensive upright for the family room. That salesperson knew how to ask motivational questions!

Analyzing Your Prospect

Do your homework. Learn everything you can about past buying motivations of your prospects' company, about their friends and neighbors, about the groups they identify with. There's nothing worse than trying to sell a house by extolling the wet bar and wine cellar, and then finding the prospect is a member of Alcoholics Anonymous . . . unless it's trying to sell a coffee maker to a Mormon (they avoid caffeine), funeral flowers to an orthodox Jew (against their customs), or a teak desk to a member of Save Our Rain Forests. Be as prepared as you possibly can before you meet your prospect.

True Story!: "IT'LL LAST A LIFETIME" To: the terminal cancer patient...

Then, in your first few minutes, you can probe for motivations with questions like these:

- What do you think you need, Alice, to get the job done?
- What do you feel is your biggest problem in . . . ?
- Mark, what's the most important thing about . . . ?
- What do you like most about . . . ?
- What do you like least about . . . ?

Follow these up with *responsive* questions:

- What would *you* suggest?
- I understand that's what they feel, but what's your opinion?
- Why is that important to you?
- What do you think is a better way?
- Then how do you feel about . . . ?
- What would be your reaction to . . . ?
- Could you tell me more about that?

Your real relationship with your prospects doesn't start until you identify and tap into their specific buying motives. Even when someone telephones and says, "Come on over—I need to buy something," you should want to be more than an order taker. An answering machine can replace you if that's all you do! Instead, turn yourself into a pro-active, advisory, *indispensable* part of the selling process. How? Ask questions!

Before each selling situation, predict what you think the buying motives will be and then ask questions that check out your assumptions. The buying motive may not always be what you think. Even if the prospect has done business with you before, something may have changed. Check it out:

- Is quality control still your major concern?
- Are you and your husband still more concerned with growth than income from your investments?
- The last time we talked you were trying a new procedure. How is that working out for you?

Take the time to fact-find. Even if nothing develops immediately, you'll still have the original order. But with a question or two, you may open the door to much, much more.

Watch for Changed Motivations

Buying motives are never fixed. A single product may appeal to a broad range of customers for many different reasons. And the same customer may buy the same product repeatedly, but with a different motivation for each purchase. People change constantly and so do their motives. Their recent experiences, temporary circumstances, or even mood may change why they buy or refuse to buy. Your research can indicate past buying motivations, but your questions establish the reasons for buying or not buying right now.

A few years ago my wife and I bought a new home. We made a careful list of all the things we wanted, the style of the house, the number and size of the rooms, the height of the ceilings, and amenities we absolutely couldn't do without. None of those things figured in our final decision. We looked at nearly a hundred houses, but each had some major flaw—too small, too expensive, wrong location. A certain fatigue and hopelessness set in. Then suddenly we saw it—the perfect house—but it was very little like our original specifications. It satisfied all our needs, but our needs and motivations had changed as we gathered more information. Your prospects go through this same process of change.

Features and Benefits: Selling the Sizzle

Human decisions are based on logic, right? If you believe this, look around you! Everything we do is related in some way to our own personal interest. Even our most selfless actions on behalf of others repay us with personal satisfaction and a feeling of self-worth. Your job is to provide each prospect with the answer to the unspoken question: "What will this do for me?"

Selling starts with features and benefits. Nearly all salespeople have had the mantra-like chant "features and benefits, features and benefits" drummed into their subconscious from training sessions. To this the professional salesperson adds one more: *motivation.* Every product or service offers the customer three things:

- Features: What the product/service is.
- Benefits: What the product/service does.
- Motivation: Your answers to the customer's question:
- "What's in it for me? How does this make my life better?"

A simplification might be: HAS—DOES—MEANS. For example, a new dish washer:

- *HAS* a video game built into the loading door. (feature)
- *DOES* provide hours of video fun for whoever is loading in the dirty dishes. (benefit)
- *MEANS* you'll never have to wash dishes again because your kids will fight to see whose turn it is. (motivation)

It's the *benefits,* not the features, that the customer is looking for, and, beyond that, the personal payoff that creates the motive for buying. Your job is to transform a feature into a benefit and from there, via the emotions, into the answer to the prospect's spoken or unspoken need.

How do features provide the desired benefits? Do people buy R-factors or B.T.U.s? No, they buy the comfort of a home that's not too hot and not too cold, and maybe lower energy bills. Do people buy insurance or cemetery plots? No, they buy peace of mind. Do people buy color TVs? No, they buy pleasure and relaxation. Do people buy automobiles? No, they buy transportation, power, speed, convenience, and status. You are not selling things. You are selling ideas, concepts, feelings, self-respect, and happiness.

Your job is to demonstrate to the prospect that the *features* create *benefits* that create a *motivation* that makes your product or service worth far more than the money it will cost. Elmer Wheeler, the great sales teacher, said: "Always sell the sizzle, not the steak." That doesn't mean that the steak isn't a great steak—nourishing, tasty, free from steroids. But your hunger for that steak is sparked by the sizzle. (That's why some restaurants serve steaks on metal plates so you can hear the meat sizzling on the metal.)

One person's benefit is another's drawback. Determine motivations and frame each feature within its perceived benefit. Then *re-question* the prospect to see if you were right:

- You'll save at least two hours a day by using this automatic sorter. That means you'll have more time to write your monthly reports for the head office. *Isn't that your biggest time pressure?* (The prospect either says "yes" or describes another more important problem.)
- Using our service will free up this entire part of your floor space. You could enlarge your showroom or have storage space for more stock. *Which of those options is more important to you right now?* (Already the prospect is imagining the new showroom in place.)
- This whole room will be much cleaner and more pleasant because of our double-filter feature. Your employees should be a lot happier and you'll save money on maintenance. *Are there any other ways a cleaner environment could help your operation?* (You are letting the prospect write her own sales talk.)

Where Do You Want to Put Your Couch?

Let me tell you how a few motivational questions sold thirty-two unbuilt condominiums in six weeks. Not only did these condos not exist yet, there wasn't even a model to show prospective customers!

The customers-but-no-condos dilemma had started just the other way around: lots of units and no customers. In the early 1970s, I was hired as a consultant by The Villages in San Jose, California, a housing development for senior citizens. They had built about 180 condo units, but only a third had sold. The remaining 120 were going at the rate of about one a week. Many of the changes I instituted involved asking questions.

First I asked myself if I would ever want to live in anything called a "Retirement Community." No! So we changed the description to a more motivational one: "Adult Luxury Living." A new advertising campaign was formulated by the ad agency, recalling the old Packard auto commercials: *"Ask the man who owns one."* Radio, TV and newspaper ads featured interviews with happy homeowners describing why they loved living at The Villages. Why were all these people willing to give testimonials? Because someone bothered to *ask* them!

Then I locked up all the model homes and took down the "open" signs. It was no longer possible to tell, driving down the street, which houses were occupied and which were empty. This ended the woebegone look of rows of unsold units. Instead of a "Scenic Drive" sign on the entry road, I had a gate put in with a guard who asked what your business was. This gave a sense of security and exclusivity.

All prospects were directed to a central buying office. There the salespeople loaded them on electric golf carts and took them on a tour of the community, asking their opinions on the pharmacy, medical center, grocery store and other amenities. (See focusing attention in Chapter 6—Presentation Questions.) As they drove, the salesperson also asked about the prospect's requirements and interests (See Chapter 5—Probing Questions) and had a chance to qualify the buyers. (See Chapter 4—Qualifying Questions.)

After the prospects had looked at a model home, the shops, and the golf course, they were driven up to the top of a hill at the center of the community from which there was a spectacular view. Standing there with the prospect, the salesperson asked the trial-close question—and I threatened to fire anyone who didn't—"Look at that view! Is there any reason in the world why you wouldn't want to live here?"

The only way prospects could say "no" to that was by offering and analyzing their own objections. (See Chapter 7—Objection Questions)

Sales jumped from one unit a week to eight. They sold so well that pretty soon The Villages ran out of houses to sell and still the buyers came. The builders decided to produce more, but it would be months before any new models would be ready to show. Management wanted to close everything down in the meantime. I advised against it.

Instead, we covered the walls of the sales office with drawings and elevations of the new houses. Outside in the parking lot I had a floor plan painted on the asphalt in exact scale. The salespeople took the prospects out and walked them through the "house." When they reached the living room, the salesperson gestured to the space and asked: "Where do you want to put your couch?" Here were people standing in a parking lot, looking at lines on the ground, but that question made them feel as if they were already in their new home, deciding where to put the furniture. That question sold the thirty-two unbuilt units as quickly as the existing houses had sold.

The Emotion Factor Equation

All decisions include an element of self-fulfillment. The professional salesperson can't afford to ignore the Emotion Factor in motivation. Let's write this as a mathematical equation—Logic and reason divided by emotion equal motivation:

$$\frac{\textbf{Logic + Reason}}{\textbf{Emotion}} = \textbf{Motivation}$$

Logic and reason ride on the horse of emotion. Prospects buy for emotional reasons and *then* back up their decision with logic and reason.

This doesn't mean that you can base your sales appeal on abusing the emotional vulnerability of your customers. Sooner or later reason will set in and they will recognize that they have been tricked. (The legal authorities may also recognize that they have been tricked.) To keep your reputation and your customers' trust, be sure in your own mind that each feature has a real, honest, and logical benefit for this particular customer. Then frame that benefit in terms that touch the emotions. Once you've done that, the prospect will provide even more reasons to support the sale. When we are emotionally committed to something, we will find all sorts of logic for our actions.

Every product or service has an emotional appeal, even if it isn't immediately obvious. For example, a computer is an electronic system that can store millions of bits of information through simple ON/OFF sequences of impulses. Do we buy this capacity? No. We buy computers to increase our business volume, our efficiency, our productivity, to make our jobs easier and our lives better while we make more money. We buy them to make us more powerful.

Obviously some logic is required to select the capabilities of a particular computer or software system to perform the functions we want. But the *need* for the computer is emotional. Look on logic and reason as the twin banks of a river of emotion that leads ultimately to a decision to buy.

Right Brain/Left Brain Decisions

There is a sound biological reason why the decision process is divided between logic and emotion. There are two spheres or sides to the human brain. The left side (for most people) is the "logical " verbal side that sorts facts and figures. The right side is the "emotional" visual side, good at organizing by size, shape, and distance. It provides the intuitive power necessary to assign values and relationships to all those facts and figures perceived by the left side of the brain. Everyone uses both sides of their brain, adjusting the balance to the task at hand. Some people are noticeably better at using numbers or at jobs that require strong spatial skills, so one half of their brain is dominant most of the time.

When you are questioning a prospect, ask questions that help you decide whether the logical left brain or emotional right brain is currently dominant. Then adjust your presentation to address the need for more logic or more emotional appeal.

For example, the prospect wants to know what something costs. Sound simple? But is it the right- or left-brain asking?

If it's a left-brain request for numbers, you offer price comparisons, statistics on return for investment, or start-up versus operating costs. But it may also be the right-brain saying "I don't know if I can afford this—I'm uncomfortable— Do I want to commit to this in view of the bigger picture?" Then you need to tie the purchase to a larger vision, picture the final result, relieve discomfort by stressing how a payment plan combined with the increased productivity will actually *reduce* monthly costs.

So to check out whether you are dealing with right-brain or left-brain concerns, you might ask questions like:

- Is the immediate cost the most important factor in your decision, or are you more concerned with the long-term value?

  Left-brain response: "Tell me the immediate costs."

  Right-brain response: "What long-term value?"

- Are you concerned that this might not be the right step for you right now?

  Left-brain response: "Give me the figures and I'll decide."

  Right-brain response: "Yes. I'm not sure how this fits in with . . . ."

Watch for clues so you don't dump lots of statistics on someone in a right-brain holistic mode or stress the relationship of your product to the prospect's long-term aspirations when he or she is operating mainly in the fact-sorting left-brain.

The Four Emotional Stages of a Sale

Every prospect goes through four stages before buying:

- Attention
- Interest
- Desire
- Action

These four stages are commonly known by the acronym AIDA. A sale boils down to leading a prospect through these mental phases.

Attention. Attention-getting questions, statements, or actions are like a drum-roll. They get attention. This is your "hook." Once you've got it, you move quickly along to arousing interest. In a good sales presentation, it should be difficult to notice where one leaves off and the next begins.

- Have you ever seen a million dollar paper clip?
- How did you build such a superb design team?
- How would you like to commute to Europe in under three hours for less than $100?

Interest. Interest is aroused by the skillfulness of your appeal to the prospect's buying motives. Decide ahead of time why this particular prospect should buy your product or service. Then use your probing questions to see if you were right.

- Do traditional paper clips ever jam your machinery?
- What's the greatest need in your design department right now?
- How are you planning to handle the 1992 regulations for the European Economic Community? How will they affect your overseas business?

Desire. After you've got the prospect's interest, you go on to create or enhance *desire.* Desire is the hunger that makes us eat. Desire is the excitement that makes us act. Your prospects won't buy until their desires make them want to buy. Create and build on the existing wants that you have exposed through your skillful questions. Use more questions to point out how the benefits will enhance them and their lives. Your prospects will then realize how much they want to buy.

- How important is it not to lose downtime on those machines because of jamming?
- If your designers had computers 20 times faster than the ones you use now, how do you think that would affect their creativity?
- If your people could visit any major European city and be back here the same day, how could that increase your business?

Action. Your final questions motivate the prospect to *action*, to become a customer. This is closing the sale. If the preceding phases have been carried out skillfully, your final step is routine—signing the order and arranging for financing and delivery.

- How many weeks would it take for these biodegradable paper clips to pay for themselves? How long do you want to wait before you switch?
- If you could have these new computers in place by April, how would that affect your fall line? Would you rather have them installed by March?
- Would you prefer to sign up for the Super-Concorde Travel Plan A or Travel Plan B? Plan A offers more savings in the long run, but do you think Plan B would be better to start with?

"But Why Do You Want to Sell?"

Wally Stabbert, president of the Institute of Certified Business Counselors, has been a broker for many years. His job is to match up people who to sell businesses with those who want to buy. "Asking questions is half the secret of success," says

Wally. "The other half is listening carefully and persisting until you have enough information to be an adviser and consultant to your client."

One of Wally's toughest jobs was trying to sell a distributorship with a tremendous client list and a great deal of good will, but only three employees and $400,000 in assets. The problem was that the owner wanted $1.5 million in cash. This business had been listed with another broker who couldn't sell it, so Wally was called in as an adviser.

Wally's first question to the owner was, "Why do you want to sell?" The owner gave all the usual reasons, but Wally kept saying, "Yes, but why do you want to sell?" Finally the owner admitted he was bored. He'd been in business for fifteen years and made a lot of money, but now he wanted to go on to something else.

"What are you going to go on to?" Wally asked. The owner didn't know, but he wanted the sale price in cash so he'd be able to move if an opportunity arose.

"If you buy another business, will you be doing it to cure your boredom or to make more money?" The owner admitted he already had enough so he must be looking for something interesting to do for the rest of his life.

"Why don't you protect your assets and your income for the rest of your life by selling this business for 30% down and financing the 70% difference yourself? That way you'll have $500,000 in cash to set up another business and $1 million secured by a business you know is successful. This would give you guaranteed income so you can concentrate on enjoying your new business." The owner thought it over and agreed.

Then Wally said, "To help us sell your business, let me ask you these questions." He pulled out a printed form. (Wally has found that an official-looking questionnaire can sometimes get more honest, truthful, and complete answers than verbal questions.) The questions on the form started like this:

- What is the best thing about your business?
- What is the worst thing about your business?
- Describe the best customer that you have.

- Describe the worst customer that you have.
- What single technique do you think has made your business successful?

He continued with similar questions until he was able to make up a list of features, benefits, and motivations to present to prospective buyers. He sold the business.

Self-Motivation

Professional salespeople have a reputation for doing *what* they should *when* they should. Why? Because they've learned to motivate *themselves* as well as their clients.

What motivates you? Are you excited about making lots of money? Is financial security your goal? Or would you love doing this job even if *you* had to pay *them?* Is self-fulfillment important? Do you want to be recognized as an achiever? Do you enjoy praise? Do you need praise? Do incentive awards—vacations, bonuses, even trophies—put you in high gear? Is competition what revs your engine? Or are you challenged by setbacks? Does a turndown crush you or does it really get your adrenaline going?

A good sales supervisor knows how to spot and use the motivations of each salesperson. One of my early bosses quickly discovered that I would double or triple my sales whenever I had a sales trainee in tow. My motivation—though I didn't realize it at the time—was that I wanted to show how smart I was! I had to prove myself, impress the newcomers I was teaching. Their wide-eyed amazement and awe were worth ten times any commission I got on the extra sales.

So ask yourself: What motivates me? Decide what supplies your gas and what puts on the breaks. Do you suffer from "sales-success block"? Is the idea that selling is somehow "beneath" you lurking somewhere in your mind? Or that it is beyond your capabilities? Does the attitude of your friends and family influence you? Are your unconscious beliefs and "attitude" going to write you a self-fulfilling scenario?

Three Questions That Deserve "No!" for an Answer

1. Do you secretly feel that you just don't have it in you to be a professional salesperson?
2. Do you believe that somehow it's *not* okay to succeed in sales? That selling is really beneath you, a demeaning occupation?
3. Do you doubt that there are enough resources available to train and support you until you reach your goal?

If any of these doubts is still plaguing you, you are going to get rid of them and change your *attitude* as you read this book. Here's a question you should be able to answer "yes!" to: Can you see yourself receiving big rewards for your professional sales results? Tom Luceder, president of Intermark, says: " . . . you have the right and duty—once you determine that your product is ethical and usable—to be passionate about packaging and selling it. If it weren't for you, this wonderful product wouldn't reach the buyers."

Now that you understand some of the motivations behind sales, it's time to start looking for prospective customers. And where do you find your prospects? You start with the process called prospecting.

"Whenever a customer explains his needs, I am very free with asking questions to be sure I understand what he is telling me: 'What you mean by that is . . . ?'"

Ed Ayd
Senior Account Manager
Dataserv

3

Prospecting Questions

"May I see the owner?"
Turned a cold call into a $72,729,340 sale to one
firm. (See page 40.)

---

*"Which apartment does the pregnant lady
live in?"*
Located more than 100 prospects. (See"page 42.)

---

*"If you were driving down the street looking
for a hotel,would you want to go into one
with such a shabby facade?"*
Sells to three out of ten cold calls with an average
sale of $4,300 each. (See page 46.)

L earning everything about selling except prospecting is
like mastering ninety-nine ways to make love and then real-
izing that you don't have a partner. Prospecting is the first and
most important step in the sales process. You can never sell
anything. You can only find a buyer. That's called prospecting.

Every sale starts with prospecting. The process can take a
few moments or a few days. If your commodity has a very
specialized use—for example a nuclear power plant—locat-
ing qualified prospects may be easy. But when your product
or service has wide use or appeal, your challenge begins.

Where do you go to find potential prospects—the people,
the companies, and the organizations who might buy? What
questions do you ask to track them down?

All salespeople, even professionals, pass right by good
prospects each day without recognizing them. New people

and companies come to town. A change in the economy makes someone more receptive to your offer. Existing customers have new needs. To be successful in the long term, take nothing for granted. Do more checking, ask more questions, and make yourself more open to new opportunities.

Never Underestimate the Basics

The intention of this book is to emphasize two things:

1. The importance of creative and adaptive questioning
2. The importance of basic questions

Creative questions are often exciting and fun, but never underestimate the importance of the basics—the questions you've asked ten thousand times in the past and will ask ten thousand times more in the future. Donald C. Scheidt, the president of Insurance Coordination Services, Inc. told me a great story that demonstrates the importance of basic prospecting:

It was 11:30 A.M. and I was south of Fresno, returning to my office from a previous call, when I saw a sign naming a fruit packaging business near the freeway. I pulled off and drove into the parking lot. I asked the receptionist the standard questions: "May I see the owner?" She said, "We have several owners. Which one would you like to see?" "Which one is in?" I asked.

That day I managed to talk to the president because it was September. In July or August, the height of their season, they would have been too busy to see anyone. The president informed me that they were considering purchasing life insurance for estate tax purposes. I should contact his accountant and provide him with the necessary proposals. I convinced the accountant that I could provide superior service and products compared to another company he was already talking to.

> *I certainly made good use of my time. As a result of that one cold call, I have sold them and their referrals $72,729,340 in insurance during the past eleven years..*

Sometimes a very ordinary question like "May I see the owner? " can result in extraordinary rewards. Don't forget the basics.

Write a Success Profile

Start by asking yourself which factors have led to success in previous sales. Analyze your past buyers, using the "who, what, when, where, why" method. Write those words across the top of a page:

Who	What	Where	When	Why
Buyer #1				
Buyer #2				
etc				

Now answer those questions for each of your previous buyers. *Who* were they? *What* did they buy? *Where* did you meet with them? *When* did you meet—what time of day, what day of the week? *Why* do you think they said "yes" to your proposal? Analyze all of these things, and you will begin to see patterns emerge.

Next look for new prospects who meet the same criteria. People or companies with desires and needs similar to your past buyers will be good prospects for your next sale. Call on them ear-to-ear (phone canvassing), face-to-face (in person), or eye- to-eye (by mail).

Where Do Prospects Come From?

The following are traditional sources of prospects.

Referrals.

The best way to find new prospects is to get referrals from people you've already sold and from people you have tried to sell. These referrals are called "hot prospects."

Company leads.

If the company you work for provides leads or a list of previous buyers, contact those names. But never depend solely on your company's leads. Why? Don't trust your future to someone else. Learn the art of prospecting for yourself.

At one time I was in a business where I provided leads through telephone solicitation to all of our salespeople. My very *top* salespeople never took a company lead. They were too busy with their own methods of prospecting. They had a successful method going, so they left company leads to the less enterprising.

At the library.

A great place to develop your own prospecting list is at the library. If you are in general sales and your product or service has a wide range of possibilities, remember that leads on new prospects can come from trade journals, industrial indexes, chambers of commerce, lists of trade and service groups, membership lists, and even daily newspapers. Become a regular reader of any related trade and consumer publications. They'll show you who is buying and selling.

At Meetings.

Join those organizations associated with your industry or its customers and attend meetings. Sit there and listen. Observe. You'll get marvelous new ideas on where to find your prospects. Won't you?

On the Street.

One of my very first sales jobs was selling baby photo albums door-to-door. I was constantly looking for new mothers. My company got birth announcements from the local newspapers and these were my leads. One day a crew of people from a competing company came to town. They informed me that they were going to put me out of business because they had arranged to get their leads directly from the local hospitals. As soon as a baby was born, they would know about it and contact the mother before I could. To solve this problem I started looking for pregnant women wherever I went. One strategy was to stop at any large apartment complex and ring the manager's bell. I'd explain that I had an appointment with a pregnant tenant, but I'd lost her name: "Which apartment does the pregnant lady live in?" Frequently the manager would respond: "Which one? We've got three..." That was three new prospects. (If the manager was a woman, I sometimes knew about the baby before the husband did!) Then I called on these prospects and explained that "since you are going to be so busy with your new baby, you may want to make this purchase now while you have time. One thing less to bother about later." It was a very successful method. I was teased a lot by my wife. She said I was the only man she knew who spent his time pursuing pregnant women.

Six Other Ways to Add to Your Prospect List

If you're not selling nuclear reactors or artificial hip replacements—if what you're selling has a somewhat broader market—go get a big sheet of paper and list the names of potential buyers.

Ask Past Clients

Your best prospects are past clients. Once people have purchased from you, they become as valuable as priceless jewels and should receive the same protection and care. A happy client will give you additional clients through referrals. Start your prospecting list with the names of all past clients and stay in touch with them on a regular basis. A handwritten note or a phone call tells your clients that you are interested in them and opens the door for additional sales.

Ask Personal Acquaintances

The second group that should demand your attention is your acquaintances. These are people you know, perhaps well,

but who aren't close to you, who aren't in your inner emotional circle. (You don't want to sell to *friends*, but you do
want them to buy from you.) When I'm thinking about hiring
new salespeople, the first thing I ask them for is a list of 200
names and address of people they know. Most people can
come up with the names of five people who think they are
terrific. But to really sell, you need to know hundreds of
people who know you, at least by sight or by name.

Many salespeople don't want to call on their acquaintances. This is a mistake. If what you're selling isn't good
enough for the people you know, then it isn't good enough
for strangers either, is it?

If it *is* good enough, start by making a list of everyone you
know and begin to think of them as potential buyers. The
names that should go on your prospecting list are those individuals who would recognize your name if they received a
telephone call or note from you. (If they are more likely to
know you by face alone, consider a business card or letter-
head that includes your photo.) Contact these people often
and, when appropriate, offer your product or service.

Ask Your Own Suppliers

The next best source is the people *you* buy from. What have
you bought recently? Go through your checkbook and credit
card receipts. List the names of the people who have sold you
goods or services and put them on your prospect list.

Ask People in Your Former Occupation

Most salespeople have had a life-before-sales. They did other
kinds of work before they went into selling. What did you do?
Hopefully you have a natural rapport with the people in those
fields. Add the names of everyone—or at least the source of lists
of names of everyone —in those fields to your prospecting list.

Ask Civic, Religious, and Social Club Members

Are you active in social clubs, service clubs, alumni associations, or at your church, synagogue or mosque? Get a list of
all the other members of these organizations and solicit them
as your prospects. Your membership gives you an identifica-

tion and an excuse for contacting these individuals. The more exposure you have, the easier it is to do business with the other members of the groups to which you belong.

Ask Perfect Strangers

Learn to be innovative in getting names for your prospecting list. Some possible sources, depending on what you sell, might be:

- Trade organization membership lists
- The Chamber of Commerce
- The public library—an excellent source for dozens of business directories.
- Building directories (in metropolitan or industrial areas)
- Faculty lists of nearby schools and colleges
- City, country or state lists of people licensed in a profession; birth, death, and marriage records; or legal records
- Today's newspaper and back issues
- The Yellow Pages
- City maps and reverse directories
- Membership lists of clubs—tennis clubs, golf clubs, model airplane clubs, gardening clubs, glee clubs, etc., etc.
- Your city's Welcome Wagon
- Industrial directories
- Dunn & Bradstreet
- Association and Corporate lists (*Million Dollar Directory, The Standard Rate and Data Guide, Encyclopedia of Associations*, etc.)

Ask Everyone

Every professional knows that "Ask everyone" is one cliche that *really* works, and every experienced professional has a story like the one Alan J. Parisse told me:

> In the early 1970s, I was strolling back from lunch with a new fellow in our firm, a young guy I was training to retail securities. He asked me, "Where do I get leads?" I said "Ask everybody." To illustrate, I pointed to the newsstand

on the corner. I had always had a good relationship with this newspaper vendor—I often
stopped to chat with him, and he knew about
my business. Some of my friends had suggested
I was crazy to waste my time, but I liked him.
So half- kiddingly I asked him, "Who do you
know who might be interested in investing some
money right now?" He looked at me thoughtfully
and said, "I have a friend who just received a
disability claim and came into a whole lot of
money . . . ." We got an investment of
$100,000 from this referral.

Keep Your Eyes Open

Often finding a hot prospect can be as simple as looking
around you. Timothy Murphy, the dynamic sales manager for
an industrial textile fabricator, finds some of his best prospects by noticing the buildings he passes:

Whenever I see a commercial building that needs a new
canopy awning, I stop the car, go in, and ask for the man-
ager/owner. I ask, "Do you realize you've got a problem? Do
you know about what they call 'street appeal'? Everything about
your building looks great except your canopy awnings. Are you
aware of the effect this can have on potential clients? If you were
driving down the street looking for a hotel in this city, would
you be comfortable going into one that had such a shabby
facade? Is there anything to identify you on this street and
make you stand out from your competition? Are you aware of
your alternatives? My job is to help you generate revenue. How
do we do this? I show you how to make the visual statement:
'Yes, my company is successful and easy to find.' "

Basically it's the FUD approach—Fear, Uncertainty,
Doubt—and I'm the fellow with the solution.

Know Everyone

A wise person knows everything; a wise salesperson knows
everyone. If you're in general sales, you should know and be

known by at least a hundred people in your industry and another hundred in your community. All their names should be on your prospect list. Even if you sell a highly specialized item like a nuclear reactor, you should know everyone in your field who may someday want to use your product. The wider your contacts, the better your reception. The better your reception, the more referrals you will get and the more you will ultimately sell.

How to Get Referrals

The only way to get a referral is to *ask* for it. No one will ever offer if you don't ask. It's not easy, but it's incredibly rewarding. Never leave a sales call, successful or not, without asking, "Who do you know who could use my service?" When people like you and your product or service, they are happy to give you a referral. Ask your friends and acquaintances. I have found that they too are very happy to help. All you have to do is ask.

Ask specifically for one referral. Direct their thinking by limiting the scope. Say:

> *If you were me and you could make only one more salescall before you retired, on whom would it be?*

When you have that name, refocus them again on another category of prospect:

> *And if you could give me the name of only one relative/neighbor/club member/coworker, who would that be?*

Tell them "I don't want your Christmas card list, just one name."

> *Who's your toughest competitor? Could I use your name if I call on them?*

Here are things you can do so that people are eager to give you a referral:

1. Have a good product or service. The best salespeople will flop if what they're selling is no good. Sell what you believe in and then believe in what you sell.
2. Be enthusiastic—for your job, your company, your life. Enthusiasm is contagious. People love to be around enthusiastic people, and they like to refer them to others.
3. Know what you're talking about. Know all about your product or service. Refine your communication skills and techniques so you can share what you know.
4. Be tactful. Tact is essential. You are an ambassador of goodwill, a diplomat handling clients and their problems. Everything you do reflects on your company.
5. Look good. Be neat, in control, appropriately dressed and groomed. You only have one chance to make a first impression.
6. Be healthy. Physical fitness is a tremendous plus. Look healthy, act healthy, and be healthy. Super salespeople work hard and need every ounce of stamina they can get so they can radiate health. Who looks forward to working with someone who is sickly, exhausted, at the end of their rope?
7. Be honest. You can never be too honest or too ethical in business. The slightest hint of sleaze or fudging—even if you claim you are doing it at the expense of your company to benefit the potential customer—will taint all your future dealings.
8. Give great service. It is impossible to repeat this too often. If other people are selling what you are selling, good service is more important than price, than fancy advertising gimmicks, more important even than having the latest technology. If the customers know you will *be there* for them when they need you, they'll stick with you and your company and give you many referrals.

What Form Do Referrals Take?

What exactly do you ask for? Here are the four basic kinds of referrals:

1. A phone introduction: "Hi, Ted. I'm giving your name to Mary McGillicudy from the XYZ company. I think she's got something that would interest you."
2. Letter of introduction: "Dear Ted: This is Mary Mc-Gillicudy. I thought you'd like to know about her product which might be useful for your new project."
3. Letter of testimony: "Dear Ted: We've had a great success using Mary's service and I thought you'd like to know about it too. We love her company's work and everything about dealing with them. " This is a powerful referral to a prospective client.
4. "Just use my name." A time saver, but be very careful with that one. It sounds innocent enough, but when people give you their good name to use you now have *two* people to lose as clients. If your referral is by phone or letter, the referrers have a chance to add their own cautions and conditions. They have passed you on and are no longer part of the equation. But with just their name, they seem to be giving you a carte blanche recommendation. Proceed as if two reputations are at stake because they are—yours and the referrer's. If you irritate or disappoint the referral in any way, the aggravation will be directed at both you and the person who referred you. Then he or she will never, *never* recommend you again.

   Extremely rare but best of all is the personal introduction—being walked down the hall to another office or being introduced at a lunch or meeting, with the referrer praising you in person to your new potential customer. You can't beat that!

   But no matter what form your referral takes, treat it like pure gold. Because it is.

Following Up on Referrals

What do professional salespeople do when they get a referral? They go into action!

1. Thank the referrer: Within twenty-four hours, write a handwritten note of thanks to the person who gave the referral.

Don't type it, don't use a form letter. Make it a little handwritten note. That personal touch sets you apart.

2. Contact the referral: Within twenty-four hours, even if you can't call on the referral directly, call, write, or do whatever is appropriate. Act immediately. There is a saying in sales: "The older, the colder." You may be wondering why you must act so quickly. After all that prospect may never have heard of you, doesn't know you're going to call them. The twenty-four hour limit has to do with *you* and your thinking. The longer you wait to move on a referral, the less important that referral seems.

3. Report back to the referrer. Within seventy-two hours let the person who referred you know that you've followed up. If anything positive happened, mention that too. This demonstrates that the referral was important to you and also demonstrates your follow-through capabilities—a valuable quality for anyone the referrer wants to do business with.

Now you've done your prospecting for names of potential clients. It's time to go on and qualify them.

"The biggest sale I ever made was sixty specialized computer systems costing $3,500 each. I was referred to the prospect by a company I had been cultivating but had never sold to. How did I get this referral? I asked for it."

Sharon Borne
Sales Representative
Project Data Corporation

4

Qualifying Questions

"Are you Catholic?"
Sold more than 50 deluxe Protestant and Catholic
Bibles a month. (See page 55.)

---

*"How much could you write a check for
right now? Not "would," could?"*
Qualified 999 out of 1,000 investment prospects.
(See page 59.)

---

*"Can you afford to take three years off to
earn an M.B.A. degree?"*
Increased responses 30 per cent and registration 25
percent. (See page 60.)

S heila, my wife and partner, set out one morning to buy a new Mercedes. She went into a Mercedes dealership, looked at the cars, sat in them, and opened and closed doors. She was ready to write a check on the spot. But no salesperson acknowledged her presence. Maybe they thought she couldn't afford a Mercedes.

When she finally located a salesman, he said, "If you see something you like, let me know" and walked away. She pursued him and started to ask questions about models. The salesman stopped her: "Why don't you bring you husband in and we can talk seriously."

Sheila stormed out, walked down the street, and bought a Cadillac from another dealer who knew how to qualify buyers. If anyone at the Mercedes dealership had taken the trouble to learn her needs and wants, had answered her questions and demonstrated the product, had made her feel important, then she would be driving a Mercedes today instead of a Cadillac.

The Mercedes salesperson forgot to qualify. Many salespeople forget to qualify.

Qualifying is finding out (through questions) if the person you have selected as a prospect (or who has selected you as a seller) has the *need* to buy, the *motivation* to buy, the *authority* to make the decision to buy, the *money* to buy, and finally the *trust* to buy this particular product or service from *you.*

You'll waste a great deal of time and grief pursuing a prospect who isn't "qualified" to be your customer. You'll also avoid missed sales when you turn away an eager, qualified buyer.

You qualify each prospect five ways:

1. Need: Is this particular prospect able to use what you are selling?
2. Motivation: Does this prospect want what you are selling?
3. Authority: Does this person have the power to make the buying decision? Do others participate in or make the final decision?
4. Affordability: Can this prospect afford what you are selling? (Or can you prove to the prospect that the savings or financial return of using your product/service will more than compensate for the cost? Can you offer a payment arrangement that lets the product/service "pay for itself" ?)
5. Trust: Does this prospect believe in you and your product?

These five qualifying factors relate to the five reasons why people won't buy what you are selling.

1. They don't *need* what you have.
2. They don't *want* what you have.
3. They haven't enough *authority* to buy.
4. They haven't enough *money* to buy.
5. They haven't enough *confidence* in you, your company, or your product.

Qualify and *re*qualify each prospect on each factor throughout the sales process. If you can overcome those five reasons during the qualifying period, then you know you're talking to a potential buyer.

Ask Before You Disqualify

Never be hasty about disqualifying a prospect. Appearances can be deceiving. The scruffiest teenager may be a millionaire pop star or computer magnate. The stereotypical "little old lady from Dubuque" may be a world-famous art connoisseur or sports car racer. Even your past experiences may prove inaccurate as a guide. Always, *always* ask questions before you decide not to waste time on an unlikely prospect.

Remember that Mercedes dealer? What should that salesman have asked that would have confirmed that Sheila was a serious buyer? Here are some possible questions that can help identify the hot prospect without offending the casual browser who may be a future customer:

1. "What can I do to help you today?" (Very slight emphasis on "today")
2. "What do you think of this color?" (Or style, feature, location, size)
3. "How does this model impress you?"

Then *listen* to the response. Is the prospect eager to ask questions? To weigh one model against another? To have you demonstrate a product? Progress to asking what factors (color/style/feature/location/size/price) are important to the prospect. Is availability or delivery time a factor? Yes? Congratulations. You've just asked yourself into a sale.

Here's another true story that also took place in a Mercedes showroom, although with a happier outcome for the salesperson. The three fellows who thought up and marketed the famous Pet Rock had offices down the hall from me at the height of the Pet Rock craze. They'd made over a million dollars with their comic toy in a very short time. One day the three of them—George Coakley, Gary Dahl, and John Heagerty—stopped by a Mercedes showroom after lunch to look at the cars. George decided he'd buy one. Not to be outdone, Gary said he'd also get one. "Me too," said John.

The salesperson decided these guys were out to lunch in more way than one. "And *how* would you like to pay for these three cars?" he asked in his snootiest manner. Gary thought a moment and pulled out his checkbook and said, "I'll get it, George. You got lunch." Fortunately for the salesperson, his customers saw the humor of the situation, but he could just as easily have lost a big sale by failing to qualify his prospects.

How Do You Pre-Qualify Buyers?

Some selling situations make it hard to qualify buyers until you are actually face to face, asking them questions—for example, in-store selling, door-to-door, or selling through office calls. But if you are selling large items, there are many aids to help you qualify. Check Dun and Bradstreet listings, industrial directories, annual company reports, and membership lists such as those of Chambers of Commerce, trade associations, and credit unions. These will give you an idea about who is qualified to buy what you sell so you can concentrate on the most likely customers.

Questions to Qualify NEED to Buy

Does the prospect have any need for what you are selling? Ask! When I approach people about hiring me for speeches and seminars, one of the first questions I ask is, "Do you ever have meetings where you hire outside speakers?" If they say "No, we never have meetings and if we ever did, we certainly wouldn't hire an outside speaker!" then I know this is probably not a hot prospect. I've *dis*qualified them as immediate buyers, worth an expenditure of time and energy. (This doesn't mean that I won't cultivate them, check back with that organization in a few months, or keep my ears open to hear if something changes.)

Examples of questions that will qualify the need to buy are:

- How many of your employees are covered by your company's insurance plan?
- What do you plan to use a copy machine for?
- How do you arrange your executive travel?
- How old is the car you're driving now?
- How often does your present model need repairs?

Sharon Borne of Project Data Corporation sells $3500 computer systems that only do only one job, bookkeeping for FHA- financed housing. That is a fairly specialized use. She uses questions like these to qualify potential buyers:

- What are your plans for using this system?
- Will you use it at every site or only at the corporate office?
- What is your time frame for setting up this system?
- What do you now do by hand and what do you do by computer?
- What do you expect to accomplish with this system?

Through this combination of open and closed questions, she can quickly identify qualified prospects.

One of my earliest jobs when I was in college was selling deluxe, beautifully bound Bibles. I carried both the Catholic Douay and the Protestant King James versions. My problem was to discover which version my prospect might prefer. The neighborhood was about evenly divided between Catholics and Protestants. I needed a qualifying question that would disclose the prospect's religious affiliation without closing the door to my sales talk. I decided to ask a prospect "Are you Catholic?" If the answer was "yes," I went right on. If the answer was "no," I would say, "Good, because I'm eager to locate Protestant families . . . " If they said they were not religious, I asked about what values they wanted their children to have. If they still disqualified themselves, I would ask if they were interested in the great books of western civilization or great paintings of the renaissance (the Bibles were illustrated). You can see that I was convinced about the quality of my product and determined to find a need that it could fill in each prospect's life.

You're probably not selling Bibles door to door, but you can still use this qualifying technique in many situations to sort your customers and their needs into categories:

- Does your company use XYZ computers? No? Good, because . . .
- Are you in charge of this department? No? That's great because . . .
- Is that an unchangeable policy with you? Yes? That's excellent because . . .

Questions to Qualify MOTIVATION to Buy

We've already covered motivation in Chapter 2. Here are a few refresher questions:

- If I were a magician and could change *anything* in your company (or situation, schedule, operations.) what would that one thing be?
- What's your priority?
- What one thing would you like *never* to have to bother about again?
- Who do you use for your messenger service when something must get there immediately? How reliable are they?
- How are you keeping up with technology? What advances do you think would help you?

Questions to Qualify AUTHORITY to Buy

Find the person who really makes the decisions. Sometimes he or she is not in the Purchasing Department. Many a good salesperson has wasted weeks or months trying to deal with the wrong person. Be bold and ask, "Who makes the final decision?" Then try to see that person. It doesn't always work, but you have to try.

When you are making a sales presentation to a group, remember that there is always one person there who will be the deciding factor, the decision-maker. Notice when people glance over at someone for his or her reaction. That's where the power is, if only the power of dissent. That's the person you have to satisfy.

- Who makes the final decision, the vice president or the purchasing agent?
- Who's in charge of quality control?
- Will you be selecting the equipment or is that done by the committee?
- Will this be separate checks?

When I was in "home sales" (that is, doing presentations to people in their homes, not selling real estate), I often made my presentations sitting at the kitchen table with the husband and wife. One of my qualifying techniques was to ask for a glass of water before I started my presentation. I wanted to see who got up to get it. If one said, *"You* go get the water, dear," that one was probably the decision maker. If the wife automatically went to get it, that indicated to me that she usually deferred to her husband. Of course if they both said, "Oh, sure . . . or would you rather have a cup of coffee or a cold beer?" then I knew I had their interest and probably the sale. Do you already know a similar power-testing technique for your prospects?

In most sales, as Ed Ayd points out, "There are only one or two people who can sign the contract but eight or ten who can kill the deal." Ed is a senior account manager with Dataserv which provides support for custom tailored computer systems and backups. Once Ed was working with a prospective west coast client that was installing equipment in 632 stores.

"It was halfway through the planning process, during a technical meeting after we had completed an initial proposal. I asked the project manager, 'What do we have to do now so we can coordinate our maintenance program with your roll-out schedule?' He told me, 'I have two directors—they don't report to me but they are in charge of maintenance.' I asked, 'What shall we do?' and he suggested a meeting with them. If I hadn't asked, we would have gone to the final proposal before these two people got involved. Then they could easily have shot us down because they hadn't been part of the decision process. They might have felt something was being shoved down their throats."

So be aware of both the decision makers and the decision breakers. You must deal with both.

Questions to Qualify MONEY to Buy

Wanting something and being able to pay for it are two different things. No matter how good you are as a salesperson, your energy is wasted if your prospect can't afford what you're selling. Financing may help, but not always.

Sometimes you have eager customers for a pre-sold product, so your energy should go into working out payment schedules that are acceptable to both the company and the prospect. I have seen commissions lost because the salesperson left arrangements for a payment plan to the prospect. Many times prospects may feel embarrassed that they don't know how to go about getting financing. Your job then is to make the arrangements while you make them feel comfortable. It is better to offer this service and have them refuse than not to offer and lose a sale. Financing is part of fulfilling your prospects' needs and wants.

- Can you think of any reason—aside from the price— that you shouldn't buy this right now? (This question can narrow down and eliminate objections and establish affordability as the only barrier to the sale.)

- We have a variety of payment plans. What were you thinking of?
- Would you prefer a lower startup price or do you want to spend a little more now so you're sure of years of trouble-free service?
- Which is better: a large down-payment with small monthly payments? Or a small down payment and larger monthly payments?

Ultimately you want to know if the prospect has enough money to buy what you are selling and is willing to part with it if the conditions are right. You can check Dun and Bradstreet ratings, credit ratings, the Better Business Bureau, but there is another astonishingly simple way: ask.

When I sold investments, I would arrive for appointments, greet the prospect, and set my briefcase down on the table in front of me, unopened. Putting my hands protectively on top of the briefcase, I'd ask: *"How much could you write a check for right now? Not would, could?"* Sometimes I had to explain why I was asking: "The reason I ask is that another of my clients wanted to invest, but had no money free right now. They would have had to sell other investments before they could purchase this one." I rarely failed to get a straight answer that saved both me and the prospect much time and wasted energy.

Questions to Qualify CONFIDENCE to Buy from You

Qualify buyers about whether they have confidence in you and your product. Do they know enough details about what you are selling? Do they believe in your sincerity? Do they accept your authority and expertise? Do they believe that your product or service is all that you say it is? This is your final hurdle. Look for signs of rapport and confidence throughout your interaction by occasionally inserting "agreement" questions.

- Do you agree that . . . ? (If they don't, you are clarifying their beliefs without losing ground.)
- Your situation seems very similar to what happened to one of my other clients. Shall I tell you how we solved his problem? (If they say "no," pause until they offer a reason. If the response indicates lack of trust, continue trust-building. If the response is a real objection, address it.)
- Can you think of any other product with a better reputation for quality and service? (If they say "no," they are giving you another chance to explain how your product is superior.)
- How would you feel about trying the plan I've recommended? (The plan has been arrived at after careful questioning about needs and wants. Here your prospects have a chance to express personal trust or distrust, whether they accept your proposal or raise additional objections.)

(See more about questions to establish trust on page 72, "Establishing Rapport.")

A Three-Question Parlay

Pacific Western University offers post-graduate business degrees with limited classroom attendance. Busy middle management people can do the majority of the work by correspondence. President Phil Forte gets prospects' attention by asking three questions:

1. Would having an M.B.A. or a Ph.D. in your specialty advance your career? (Almost everyone answers yes.)
2. Can you afford to take three years off so you can go to college for a degree? (Almost everyone answers no.)
3. If I could show you a way to complete the required classes for your degree by correspondence at your own pace, would you be interested? (Almost everyone answers yes.)

At that point he explains how the university's program works and the cost. They have had a tremendous success record with thousands of people earning degrees through P.W.U.

Qualifying by Phone

How can you be sure you have a good prospect? You may be able to qualify them on the telephone. Let me show you a qualifying-question process I use when I "cold call" prospects on the telephone.

BB: Hi, I'm Bill Bethel. I'm a professional speaker and I have a couple of questions I'd like to ask you.

(I turn that statement into a question by pausing for two seconds. If the prospects don't object, that means they are willing to hear my questions. If they say, "Sorry, I'm too busy . . ." or "I'm in a meeting," I ask "When shall I call you back?" If they say "We get so *many* inquiries . . . " I ask if I can send some literature. If they say "Sorry, not interested" and slam down the phone, they have disqualified themselves.)

BB: Do you ever have meetings where you hire outside speakers?

PROSPECT: Yes.

(If a prospect says they have no meetings, the conversation is over. If they say they use no outside speakers, I ask if they would consider the fresh approach that outside speakers can bring. Occasionally a prospect will say "We only hire through the XYZ Bureau." I compliment them on their high standards, then explain that the "exclusive" booking arrangement of XYZ keeps them from hearing dozens of top speakers who aren't XYZ clients. "Would they consider . . . ?")

BB:	My subjects are sales, quality service, and personal success. Do you ever hire anyone in those areas?
PROSPECT:	Yes.
	(If prospect says "no," I ask what subjects their speakers usually cover, then—if appropriate—I explain how one of my subjects could be adapted.)
BB:	When is your next meeting? If I send you my literature today, do you promise to read it?
PROSPECT:	Yes.
	(The prospect who says "no" at this point is disqualified, but no one ever has.)

Then I follow-up with another call:

BB:	Did you get my literature? Have you had a chance to read it?
PROSPECT:	Yes.
	(If Prospect says "no," I ask when I can call back.)
BB:	Good. Now, what must I do to get you to hire me for your next meeting?

Qualifying in Person

Sometimes qualifying can't really be done until you are face to face. In-person qualifying is easy to arrange if you work in any business where prospects walk in off the street (stores, offices, showrooms, etc.) or where you confront them unannounced as they go about their daily lives (street vending, product demos at events, etc.)

But what about selling situations where you need to sit down with the prospect? Usually you need an appointment. How do you get one? Start by *asking* and expecting to get one.

How to Get an Appointment

By telephone. One way is to call and ask for an appointment. Does that sound elementary? You'd be surprised how many people get through to the person they want to see and then forget to ask "May I see you on Thursday at 4:00 o'clock?" Few prospects will volunteer their time. You *have* to ask.

By writing. Write and ask for an appointment. You can do this in several different ways:

1. A letter of introduction sent in advance by your company. It gives you credibility when the head of your department or company thinks enough of you to do this.
2. Your own letter saying that you want to meet on such and such a date, and that you will call in a few days to confirm the appointment. That's very strong.
3. A handwritten note saying "I'd like to see you." It's not as formal as a typed letter and can make the prospect feel special. Very few people in this world receive a handwritten note saying "I know your time is valuable, but if I could have five minutes I believe I could show you something that will . . . ."

Ask if you can meet with them on either of two dates. That creates a multiple-choice question. When you ask simply "Can I see you?" the answer is usually "no." Whatever kind of letter you send, you might enclose your company literature.

By cold-call. Just drop in. When you do, dress as if you expect the interview. Look like a professional. That can vary depending on your location, product, and client. If you sell milking machines or oil rig drills in the Midwest and demonstrate your product, you're going to look pretty silly "dressed for success" in an expensive suit and tie. And you probably wouldn't walk into a corporate headquarters in New York City wearing overalls and wading boots. When I say dress your most professional self, that means for the circumstances. Being professional means you fit in.

When you walk in, act as if you expect to see your prospect. For example:

- WEAK: May I see Ms. Evans?
- BETTER: Please tell Ms. Evans that Walter Bishop is here.

Do you see the subtle difference? When you sit down to wait, sit with an air of expectation. Don't settle back in that comfortable chair as if you are going to stay for the weekend. Look alert and ready.

Now you've expected to get in. You've dressed for the occasion. Your language reflects your expectation. What else can you use to help you get to see the prospect? Suppose the receptionist or secretary has some questions for you.

QUESTION:	Ms. Evans is very busy. Can her assistant help you?
ANSWERS:	No, I don't believe so, but I'll be happy to make an appointment.
QUESTION:	What do you want to see Ms. Evans about?
ANSWERS:	It's about the letter I sent her. (If you did.)
or:	I'll be happy to tell her myself.
or:	I'm the person Sam Smith referred her to. (Sam Smith is the colleague of Ms. Evans who gave you her name.)

Other responses, depending on your reading of the situation, could include "I'm here to solve her biggest problem" or "I'm here to show her how to win the Malcolm Baldrige Award for Excellence."

Qualified Candidates

Qualifying a potential customer is a process that never stops. You're going to continue asking qualifying questions all through the selling steps. For now you've got a qualified prospect and you're about to start your probing questions.

"Questions are the foundation to any selling process, the most direct route to understanding what your prospect or client is looking for. We do consultive selling, so the level of sophistication of our clients dictates good listening skills and preparation of teaching questions. The planning stage is a critical part of the selling process. You need to develop your questions and provide a context for asking them. One of the mistakes that a lot of salespeople make is to get so wrapped up in their own subject matter and expertise that they forget to provide the context for the question."

Bob Denman
Account Representative

5

Probing Questions

"What would your life be like if you didn't have to do all this yourself?"
Sold 280 interconnecting library computer systems.
(See page 70.)

"Are your customers having a hard time finding your temporary entrance with the street all dug up like that?"
Sold $6,200 worth of customized signs.
(See page 77.)

"By the way, how do you get your daily deposits to the bank?"
Increased banking courier service staff from one to eight employees. (See page 83.)

"**W**hen a customer calls up and says 'I want to order such-and-such,'" says Kevin Barry of the Oracle Corporation, "it's nice to be able to fill out the order form and say 'Sure, here you go.' But more often than not, you've *got* to ask: 'Why? How are you going to use it?' If you don't probe, if you allow a customer to buy something that's not right, they may end up frustrated or worse. Then you'll miss out on future sales down the road."

Probing means discovering your potential customer's needs and wants. You'll use probing questions throughout the selling process, but especially now before you go into your presentation. With good probing, professional salespeople move to a consulting position where they and the prospects become partners, conferring on something of mutual importance. "At the first meeting," says Allison Wilson, "I try to listen as much as I can." Allison is a Sales Service Executive with CNN.

> *I keep it as simple as possible: Who? What? When? Where? How? Are you trying to grow? What have you done in the past? Where have you tried to reach customers? Why do you think this target audience is best? Have you considered reaching a younger or older audience? I find out what their goals are and then close in.*

At this stage your questions are also a great device for getting attention and holding interest.

There's another advantage to questions. To answer them, prospects must stop whatever they are doing or thinking and focus on you and your question. Most people can't think of other things while answering questions.

The 3-Ds of Probing

Probing questions follow a 3-D format:

- Define
- Develop
- Decide

Your questions lead prospects to *define* their needs, *develop* solutions, and then *decide* how to implement them.

1. Define the problems and needs
    a. Ask about the current situation.
    b. Ask about the prospect's needs and problems.
    c. Point out other needs and problems you observe through questions so client will recognize and possibly reframe or redefine needs.
    d. Agree on the needs and problems to be worked on.

- So improving that is your major concern right now?
- Do you think employee satisfaction contributes to productivity?
- Which is more important to you right now—gross revenue or bottom-line profit?
- Does customer satisfaction help you to make more money?
- You really understand your business, don't you?
- Could you tell me more about that?

2. *Develop* possible solutions
   a. Ask about decision-making criteria: price, quality, delivery time, quality/value ratio, and reliability of service.
   b. Ask client for possible solutions.
   c. Through questioning, lead prospect to admit that your product or service fulfills most or all of the criteria.
   d. Ask if there is any reason why your product or service shouldn't be selected to fill those needs.

   - Could you give me an example of what you mean by more productivity? How would you measure it? What would represent "success" to you?
   - Is down-time a problem with that equipment? How do you handle it?
   - Could you think of a better way to deal with that?

3. *Decide* how to proceed.
   a. Ask for confirmation.
   b. Outline each other's tasks and responsibilities: "So you're going to have that ready by May 1st?"
   c. Work out an implementation schedule. "Would you like to start a week from Tuesday?"

   - Will ten work stations be enough for this department?
   - Which payment plan would work best for you? So that's the one you want to implement? What date do you want to make the first installment?

- I agree to have half the units delivered by the first of the month, right? The rest will come two weeks later, right? And you agree that the signed contracts and the 10% down payment check for $10,000 will be at my office by Friday at 5:00pm, right?

"What Would Your Life Be Like?"

"My biggest sale started out in a mundane way," says Joan Frye Williams. She is a regional representative for Inlex, Inc. which computerizes library systems. Joan told how skillful probing landed her a landmark sale:

> *A school district with 280 schools was considering automation and had been looking at individual systems for each school. The question I used to get them thinking a different way was, "What would your life be like if you didn't have to manage all this, if someone else took care of it?"*
>
> *That led them to think about centralizing the purchase. First I sold them a one-year pilot system for four schools. They agreed that if that was a success, we would have the account for the entire district with 280 schools.*

Joan recognizes that some librarians can feel threatened by the rapid takeover of their ancient profession by twenty-first century technology.

> *Early in the process I check out their feelings and help them see the benefits of purchasing from me by asking things like:*

- What do you hope will happen when you automate?
- Why are you automating?

- What kind of results are you looking for?
- How will automating your services benefit your customers?
- Was it difficult for you to get the process rolling?
- What do you think is going to happen next?

I ask about their fears and uncertainties:

- What's the worst thing you think might happen?
- Who have you been talking to and what have they been telling you about automation?
- What have you heard about Inlex?
- How would you characterize the way you feel right now?
- What's going on?

When we've established rapport, I go on to the facts:

- Who will make the final decision?
- Who has the money?
- Is the project funded?
- When is the money available?

I need to ask very few questions about functionality or product features because the library community is very functionally oriented. However, I do need to confirm their thinking about what they think they want. There is a lot of hearsay among technically naive buyers— they've heard tell somewhere that something is good, but they don't know why. I need to find out if they've thought through what they need. When we get into that mode, my most frequent question is, "What is that going to do for your library service?"

Your Opening Question

Your first probing question must capture attention, position you in the prospect's mind, establish rapport, and open the door to more questions. A tall order, yes? But a poor question can get you in trouble in the first five seconds. A typical opener from an inexperienced salesperson is "Well, how do things look today?" or "How's business?" What if business is lousy? What if the prospect's personal life is a disaster? Like a good lawyer, never ask a question that might produce an answer you don't want to hear. Your questions should always be designed to lead the prospect to the answers you want.

Of course you can ask any question if you're prepared to deal with the possible answers. One super salesman, Bob Davis, asks "How's business?" and uses a resounding negative to make a sale. Bob is manager of Field Sales Services for the Miller Brewing Company. Here's how he does it:

Bob: How's business?
Prospect: Last night was just horrible!
Bob: How are your Tuesday's normally?
Prospect: Well, they're usually slow, but last night was really bad.
Bob: Why do you think that was?
Prospect: Maybe because of the holiday last weekend.
Bob: Well, I can't do anything about last night but Labor Day is coming up and if the pattern holds, that's going to be bad for you. How about if we put together a promotion for you to draw some traffic into the store?

So you can risk any question if you're prepared with a strategy for turning your prospect's perceptions around.

Establishing Rapport

You've probably bought many things from people you'll never see again, from nondescript faceless people, even from people you actively disliked. Rapport with a customer isn't necessary for a sale, but professional salespeople know it is essential for a selling relationship. From the moment you encounter a prospect, in person or on the phone, you start trying to build a rapport: "You and I are alike in some way, therefore I can really appreciate your needs and wants."

Meeting a prospect in their home or office can give you a wealth of subjects for rapport-building. Look around for photos, art work, trophies, awards, evidence of a hobby, an area of personal or civic interest:

> *Are those pictures of your children? How old? (Mine are about the same age. Maybe they know each other.) What high school did you go to? (I went there too. OR: I know someone who went there. Maybe you know her? OR: We used to play them in the regional basketball tournaments. How are they doing now?) What year did you graduate?*
>
> *What's your golf handicap? Do you still bowl? Does your child play in Little League?*
>
> *Is that painting by Hockney? (What do you think of his latest work? OR: Oh, your wife picked it out? Is she a collector? OR: Oh, it's part of the corporate art collection? Does your firm do a lot to help the arts?)*
>
> *You like jelly beans too! Are these are from that little shop next to the jewelry store . . . ?*
>
> *Oh, have you been to Spain? On vacation? For a conference? Did you like it? Where do you plan to go next time? Does your trade association often do international conferences?*

Some big corporations, seeking a uniform look, have banned personal photos and mementos from desks and walls in their offices. Whatever you may think of this policy, it can make connecting with a stranger more difficult. Lodge pins, school rings, old school ties, and political buttons are rare these days but may offer a hint. If there absolutely isn't a clue to the person's background, try a neutral question like "Isn't this weather something?" Rain or shine, the response may give you something to build on.

Make a connection, but don't seem calculating about it. Phony bonhomie can be a big turnoff. Ron Von Trapp says, "Nothing turns me off faster than a sales rep who sits down and asks the typical questions about the fish on the wall or how long have you been here—and then jumps directly into the sales presentation. I think to myself 'You haven't earned the right to sell me.'" Ron is director of North American Sales with the Plus Development Corporation.

But simple, old-fashioned rapport-establishing questions can work on the most sophisticated prospect. Bob Davis of the Miller Brewing Company told me another great story that illustrates the point:

> Sooner or later every salesperson in the world runs into buyers who are out to prove how important they are. Mine was the buyer for a major grocery chain. The first time my chain manager and I called on him, we had a nine o'clock appointment. We got there fifteen minutes early and didn't get to see him for over an hour. Then five minutes with him and we were out the door again. Nothing happened.
>
> The second time we were caught in traffic, got there at 9:05, and he wouldn't see us because we were late. This was part of his routine to humble salespeople. The manager and I decided to get some background information on the guy. We found out that he loved sports. The next time we got into his office, instead of doing our sales pitch, I said, "What about those Bears?!"
>
> Well, we were there for twenty-five minutes while he told us about the Bears. Then we spent five minutes on business. From then on, every

> *time we'd call—which was ten times a year—
> other people would have to wait because we'd
> be in there with him for an hour. We discussed
> sports, kids, everything under the sun, because
> we had finally established a common ground
> through that one question, "What about those
> Bears?" Even though that buyer is no longer
> there, that company is still our number one or
> two client in the area.*

Bob stresses that you need to research your prospects:
"You must have *some* idea of your audience when you ask
questions. On cold calls, try to find things they are interested
in. *Talk about the prospect's concerns, not yours.*"

Uncovering Unrecognized Needs

Sometimes we don't know what we are going to say until we
hear ourselves say it. Kelly Gutierrez, Organizational Sales
Representative for Knott's Berry Farm in southern California,
finds questions a valuable way to help her prospects discover
their own feelings and beliefs:

> *Questions can uncover information that your
> prospect isn't aware of yet, develop ideas that
> haven't really been thought out. Questions can
> help you spot dissatisfaction or show you how
> you can do something better. When you ask
> interesting questions that provoke thought on the
> prospect's part—even if you're irritating them at
> first— if you hit the right question and get them
> talking to you, then you've got them in your
> court. The longer you keep them there, the
> better chance you have to make the sale.*

Kevin Barry, Sales Expeditor with the Oracle Corporation,
also uses questions to stimulate his prospects' thinking:

You deal all the time with your own product or service, but your prospects aren't familiar with it and don't know what to ask you. Your own questions can bring up ideas they haven't had time to think of. Good questions speed them up and lead them down the correct path to their end goal.

Getting the Customer Involved

Professional salespeople know that getting the prospect involved is the best way to make the sale. How do you get them involved? You ask a question that deals with them personally. It puts them in the picture while establishing rapport.

A realtor I know, Howard Marans, is an expert at this. When I bought a house from him in 1968, he started asking questions as soon as we walked into his office. He continued asking in the car and as we looked at each prospective house. He listened to learn all about our lifestyle, our family, our likes and dislikes. How would we enjoy the different features at each house?

I love a fire on a cold night. Do you? Would you be putting in a gas log or do you prefer burning real wood? Will this be Bill Jr.'s room or Tom's? Can't you see this room decorated for little Julie?

Do all the children swim? This swimming pool would be perfect for summer entertainment, wouldn't it? This patio area is perfect for summer get-togethers. Can't you smell the steaks on the barbecue?

I know you play the piano. Where do you think you would put your piano? Do you have a lot of relatives visit you? Look, two ovens and one of the new Radar Ranges that cooks with sound waves. Isn't that perfect for big parties and getting everyone together for the holidays?

The youngsters could even have a separate table over there where you can keep an eye on them while you adults talk . . . .

As he showed each house, he used all the information he had gathered to ask questions that got us involved. How can you get your prospect involved? What questions can you ask that let the prospects see themselves using your product or service?

Ron Von Trapp of Plus Development Corporation uses questions to get his prospects to work for him. "I ask them what they are trying to accomplish. Then I ask them who in their organization can help us get the information we need to come to a conclusion that we both agree with. I ask a lot of questions about who can help us get this done."

Defining Needs and Wants

After your opening, your next questions should determine the present situation and then establish the prospect's thinking about needs and wants. Defining is the first of your "3-Ds." Your prospect may think everything is great. Your job is to determine the actual situation.

A sign salesperson I know drove through a neighborhood where the streets and sidewalks were being ripped up. With a flash of inspiration, she did cold calls on several of the neighborhood businesses and asked if their customers were having trouble parking and finding their temporary entrances. Yes, indeed, this was a big problem! They were losing business but hadn't figured out what to do. She promptly sold many customized signs that apologized for the inconvenience and directed customers to parking and entrances. She had spotted a possible problem. Then with probing she either drew the prospect's attention to the problem or confirmed that the prospect knew a problem existed. With more questioning she led each business to the solution of using her signs. Everyone benefited mightily.

Your prospect may already be aware that something is
wrong. You may spot the problem immediately, but you'll
probably fail if you offer a solution before you've clarified the
problem and the need in the prospect's mind. Let the prospect discover the need and then decide on the solution. Instead of battling the prospect until you've won a sale, take the
position of supporter and adviser. Show you care about the
outcome, not just writing up a sale today. Dr. Anthony Alessandra and Phil Wexler, authors of the great book, *Non-Manipulative Selling*, put it this way:

> *People buy services or products most often be-
> cause they feel that they and their problems are
> understood by the seller. They don't buy be-
> cause an insistent salesperson makes them un-
> derstand the product.*

To use a more personal metaphor, which kind of doctor
do you want to go to: the one who examines you for fifteen
seconds, hands you a sheet of instructions, and departs—or
the one who listens to all your symptoms and fears, explains
the alternative treatments, and then designs a special regime
of medication, diet, and/or exercise based on your input?
Which treatment regime would you be most likely to follow
faithfully? Which doctor would you go back to if the first
prescription didn't work?

Developing Solutions

Probing means you start by understanding the customer's
problems, not by making the customer understand your product. There is an overwhelming and very natural human impulse to grasp the problem from a few details and jump in
with a solution before the prospect has finished describing it.
Don't!

Force yourself to continue ending your sentences with
question marks! When you spot a problem, ask questions to
confirm that the client sees it as a problem.

- Do you think that employee turnover is too high for this department? (Prospect may reply "No, it's not bad—we can live with it" or "Yes, it's our major problem.")
- You seem to have a lot of returns. Do you see quality control as a problem? (Prospect may reply, "Yes, we've got to turn this around!" or "No, we've figured the cost in already.")

As a professional salesperson, you never try to solve the problem for the customer. Simply describe possible solutions, then let the client solve it with your consultative help. Lead your customers to where *they* make a decision reflecting the problem you have helped them identify and the solution options you have laid before them. When it's their own decision, they are far more likely to be convinced of its soundness and prepared to defend it. Your proposal, which they might have been inclined to challenge, has now become their own decision to uphold.

Everyone resents feeling manipulated or coerced into a decision. If you impose your solutions on your clients, they will resent both you and your suggestions, no matter how flawless your reasoning and how good the results. It's your job to see that prospects have mentally worked through the problem to its intelligent solution so that their decisions will make both them and you happy in the future.

Suppose you are discussing a microfilm storage system with the administrator of a small city. The initial costs of equipment and transferring existing files to electronically retrievable microfiche seem quite beyond the city's limited budget. The city is committed to leases on storage space for its files. The workers who retrieve the files are very resistive to any change, and since this is a close community their opinion is very important.

Your goal is not to sell the city a sophisticated system it can't afford and might not be able to use effectively. Instead you want to see how your product may be able to help now and/or in the future.

- How much storage space do you use now? How soon will you need more?
- Do you discard some files after a certain period of time to save space? Does this ever present a problem? How do you decide what to discard?
- How many additional feet of storage space do you anticipate needing in the next year? In the next ten years?
- What is your cost per square foot for storage?
- How long does it take to retrieve a file? Does retrieval time ever cause a problem? How?
- Do you ever run into problems because a file is lost or mislaid?
- Who currently retrieves needed files? How many hours do do you think they spend? What does it cost the city? If they didn't have to do this job, what could they do instead with the time saved?
- Do you have to pay any extra for fire insurance on the storage areas? Have you had to install a sprinkler system? What if the files got wet—what would you do to dry them out? What about maintaining the space? Do you use city workers or outside services to guard, clean, and make routine repairs?
- Do you pay for heat in winter and air conditioning in the summer in the storage areas? How is heat and cold affecting the deterioration of the acid-based papers? (All commercial paper since the 1890s has been made with acid and self-destructs after a few decades.) Do you have any conservation plans for older files? Do mice, mildew, or fungus represent a problem?
- What do file boxes cost? How many new boxes do you project buying each year? Metal or acid-free cardboard?
- Are there any other costs? For example, could the city lose government funds or face penalties because it is too difficult to collect information for filing federal forms on time?
- What if the files were destroyed in a fire? What problems would the city face? How would you try to resolve them?
- How much overall do you figure it costs the city to store documents? What percentage of the city budget does this

represent? Is that about what you'd like to spend or is it out of proportion to the use you get from the files?

- Would having multiple copies of city files stored in different locations be convenient? Would it be a valuable safety measure?
- Suppose each city department could have all their files for the last 100 years stored in a unit smaller than a book?
- What if a document reader could be attached to your existing desktop computers so that each employee had immediate electronic access to files?
- Are any city documents confidential? What security measures would you need to maintain this confidentiality?
- What kind of training would your employees need to use the electronic system? Would employees who now retrieve files from the warehouse need new assignments? How could they be involved in a new system? Are there hidden human costs involved here? How would you handle personnel issues?
- Now we can figure the cost to the city of an electronic retrieval system, based on your needs . . . Looking at these figures, how would the costs of a new system be offset by current costs?

Making Decisions

You have just used questions to lead the city administrator through a complicated planning and decision process. Will you make a sale? Probably. Your questions will continue as you and the administrator decide on immediate and long-term measures, a payment plan, and implementation schedule. Your questions will reveal whether the city council must approve the expenditure, how contracts are granted, what training your company should be prepared to offer, and so forth.

But even if you don't make a sale today, you have still shown the administrator that you are acutely aware of the pressures, problems, and decisions that he or she faces. You now know the personal issues involved, the personalities, politics, and plain old procrastination that must be dealt with. You've become an ally, the one who will be consulted as soon as the budget eases, the anti-technology sentiment lessens, or the problem worsens.

Notice that in the final step of the probing encounter described above, you explained the features and benefits of your product and showed how they could meet the needs of the city. And you did it all with questions.

The Right Time for Questions

Dr. Tom McDonald believes he lost his biggest potential contract by not asking the right questions at the right time. He is president of Tom McDonald & Associates, consultants and trainers in La Jolla, California. Tom had been called in by the president of a large computer company. When he arrived, the president summoned the company's vice presidents to his office and said "Give this man ten minutes of your time." Tom met with each vice president separately. Afterward, instead of asking some very pointed questions about what the president wanted to happen, Tom went back to his office to prepare a written evaluation. He planned a one-year program for the firm, including a three-month diagnostic phase, and sent it to the president. The president never called back. What had he done wrong? His post-disaster analysis is this:

> *Each vice president was seeing me only because the president had asked them to. No one knew why I was there or what our program was. I hadn't asked the right questions up front. I should have asked the president if I could ask several questions before I spoke with the vice presidents?*

- What are your needs right now?
- What do you really want to accomplish?
- What can I do specifically to help you reach your goals?

- Can we discuss my fees and come to an agreement on how much time you will need to implement my program if you like it?

I didn't get the consulting contract because I didn't ask those questions. You must ask the right questions at the right time.

Dr. McDonald recommends that all consultants try to get answers to questions like these before they spend time preparing a proposal:

1. What does your product or service really do for your customer?
2. What are the key concerns of your customer after the purchase?
3. How can the customer get in trouble by buying your product or service?
4. What could annoy your customer about your product or service?
5. What are the short-term business and personal objectives of your customer?
6. What are the long-term objectives?
7. What are the concerns and priorities of your customers' bosses concerning your product or service?
8. Is your customer concerned about the opinion of anyone else? If so, what are the priorities of these other people?

The Right Question at the Right Time

If depositors sometimes have a hard time getting to the bank, what about a bank that would come to them? Juan Jimenez, executive vice president of the San Jose National Bank, reasoned that the bank of the future needed to go to its customers. He devised a system of courier-tellers who can pick up and record customers' deposits at their offices and stores. His problem was how to sell this new idea to clients and potential clients. His solution was a simple question: "How do you get your daily deposits to the bank?"

The San Jose National Bank started with one courier. Now a large portion of their business is handled by these traveling tellers. They have eight in the field versus three on the floor of the bank. The first couriers were college students, but they tended (understandably) to vanish during final exams and summer vacations. Now Juan employs retired professionals—school principals, teachers, and people from the electronic industry in Silicon Valley. They collect deposits from medical and real estate offices, CPA's, and manufacturers. They pick up and deliver every kind of financial document—checks, vouchers, notes, letters and documents that need to be signed, letters of authorization—everything but cash. They arrive in unmarked cars, dressed in professional attire.

Juan has just begun training them in cross-selling. They study the bank's products—checking, savings, C.D.'s, and the different types of loans and trusts. Each courier is paired with a bank officer who is always available by telephone and who can go out with the courier to set up new accounts or handle unusual situations. Each courier-teller is now a salesperson for the bank.

Five Systems With One Blow

You never know when you'll strike gold with "routine questions." When Kevin Barry was with Lanier copiers, he had a long-time client who was just about due for a new copy system. He called to tell her about a year-end special. While they were talking, he asked, "How are your other locations doing?" He learned that they were about to open two new stores.

Then Kevin asked, "Would it be beneficial for you to buy their systems now at this sale price?" With these two questions he discovered a need and parlayed a single-unit sale into five units:

> *By asking about the rest of their business, we saved them thousands of dollars and the time and energy needed to select copy equipment at*

each location. We also got a great sale. Just a little bit of probing and the larger sale opened up in front of me.

You can ask probing questions both before and during your presentation—before to assess your prospect's needs and during to confirm if you are right. Now let's look at how questions move you through your entire sales presentation.

During a call, I am constantly checking in with the prospects to clarify and confirm my understanding. Sometimes they assume you know their buzz words and acronyms. To earn the right to explore further, I summarize periodically and say "this opens up some interesting possibilities. Do you mind if I ask a few more questions?" I keep it as interactive as possible so I don't appear to be a probing machine.

Toni Gattone
Owner
Toni Gattone &
Associates

Presentation Questions

"Has your group ever played night golf?"
Helped book thousands of guest rooms for
organizations that chose *not* to schedule a night golf
event. (See page 92.)

---

*"What would you do if your roof started
leaking in the next rain storm?"*
Generated 300 roof repair jobs per month.
(See page 101.)

---

*"Have you ever wondered why some
businesses fail?"*
Generated more than $30 million in yearlysales.
(See page 103.)

You can't sell anyone anything. You can only lead people to a buying decision:

*Those convinced against their will
Are of the same opinion still.*

Questions are among the best tools in your presentation kit. When you handle them successfully, they can outperform all the glossy brochures, visual displays, and samples you can come up with. The inexperienced salesperson shows and tells and tells and shows until the prospect becomes apathetic or antagonistic. The professional salesperson knows that to keep the prospects' attention, you must ask more than you tell.

My old friend Alan J. Parisse puts it this way:

It's not just asking questions. It's really wanting the answers. There are a lot of salespeople out there who have learned the techniques of questioning, but they come off as "canned" and not really caring because they're not interested in the reply. You ask questions to know a person better because you are really interested, not just to find a hole in their defenses to ram your product through. You do ask so that you can really serve them. You ask because you are really interested.

Skillful questioning draws prospects out and leads them to decision-making. When they make the decision to buy themselves, they commit themselves to the soundness of that decision and are prepared to defend it. Instead of challenging the salesperson's proposal, prospects now see it as their own idea.

There are three kinds of questions you'll be asking as you progress through the three steps for developing and delivering your presentation:

Step 1.   Preparation: the research questions you'll ask others
Step 2.   Planning: the questions you'll ask yourself
Step 3.   Presenting: the questions you'll ask your prospects

Let's look at each step and see how professional salespeople progress from wanting to make a sale to closing a sale—ringing up the cash register or getting a signature on a contract.

Professional selling is 90 percent preparation and 10 percent presentation. Before you face your prospect, plan exactly what you want to happen. "Winging it" is never as effective as a designed presentation, although you always want to *look* unrehearsed. You are relaxed because you are well prepared.

STEP 1: PREPARATION

How do you do your homework? What do you need to find out? What's the best way to get the information you need? Professionals expect to be successful in their sales effort, but that doesn't mean they count on positive thinking alone to make a sale. They base their expectations on careful preparation well before the sales contact. Just like a good lawyer, the professional salesperson prepares adequately in advance before facing the judge—in this case the prospect.

Your planning may take a few minutes or several days, depending on who your prospect is, what you want to accomplish, and the nature of your product or service.

What Do You Need to Know About Your Prospects?

Find out everything you can about your prospects in advance, their vital statistics, business background and objectives, problems, conflicts, biases, prejudices, goals, and aspirations. If possible, fill out a personal profile.

How do you get this information? There are a variety of possible sources:

- Published profiles
- Newspaper, trade publications, and magazine articles (Keep up with current issues and check the *Reader's Guide* and newspaper indexes at your local library for back information)
- Who's Who and industry guides
- Personal feedback from prospects' colleagues, competitors, secretaries, suppliers, and customers.
- Personal observation

What are your prospect's needs, wants, prejudices, beliefs? What is most important to them? What will your product or service do to benefit the prospect?

Prepare a dossier (or at least a file card) on each prospect and update it regularly. This requires a special sort of discipline on your part because professional salespeople want to think big, not get bogged down in paperwork. But they have learned which details count, which "dues" have to be paid to be a truly effective salesperson.

What Do You Need to Know About Your Product or Service?

That's easy. Everything. More than everything. Study every detail of your product or service until you know them all backwards and upside down. Then study your competition so you can knowledgeably compare what you're selling to what they're selling.

Once you know as much as possible, avoid the all-too-human temptation to show off in front of your prospects. Firmly resist the impulse to rattle off lists of parts, complex technical explanations, or time tables. In your enthusiasm, if you get caught in the "telling" trap, you'll probably fail to notice the glazed look in your prospect's eye.

How can anyone *not* be fascinated by all those details you've worked so hard to memorize? Well, imagine that you go to a doctor with a rash and he starts telling you all the possible causes. Soon he is striding excitedly back and forth in front of you, enumerating dozens of potential treatments and outcomes, totally engrossed in proving what a brilliant medical education he has had. You and your rash are no longer center stage. How do you feel? That's just how a prospect feels when you try to impress and dazzle with your knowledge, when you try to prove your own importance. Learn to make your *prospects* feel important by listening and then supplying the relevant facts for *them*. Keep the spotlight on your prospect.

STEP 2: PLANNING YOUR PRESENTATION

The form of presentations rarely varies. You start by promising a benefit. Elaborate with an example. Explain. Ask questions. Show how what you're selling has helped others. Apply the benefits to a specific problem of the prospect's. Back up your statement with proof. Show how a loss could occur if the product or service is not purchased. Ask to be sure the prospect understands. Reemphasize the benefits. Ask for the order. Those are the elements of a good sales presentation.

What Are the Features and Benefits?

What are the characteristics—the features—of your product or service? How could they benefit your prospects? Take a sheet of paper and write all the features, positive and negative, on the left. Then list every possible benefit on the right. A technical feature that translates as "faster than our competition" could produce a list of benefits like "more convenient— saves time," "less frustrating," "increased income because more productive," "more fun," "accomplishes unpleasant task, releasing user for recreation," "gives user status among peers," etc. Naturally you'll phrase these benefits in more personal terms: "Imagine never having to wait in line again!" or "Your biggest competitor installed this improvement two months ago and they've already doubled their output."

Feature	*Benefits*
This pen has a floating ball head	It writes smoothly and ball head doesn't slip.
R-19 30-grade double poly insulation	Your family will stay cool in summer and warm in winter.
Carbide-tipped dovetailing router bits	Unlimited creativity for your woodworking projects
Extra horsepower and drag-free blades.	Fields of waving wheat
Designer-label jacket	Style, status, confidence
Hand-tied springs and goose-down pillows	Luxurious comfort at the end of a hard day

| 600,000 words defined, with complete etymologies | Sense of knowledge and power when writing, freedom from derision for making errors |
| A six-month health club membership | Health, attractiveness, business and social contacts |

Remember that you aren't selling *things.* You're selling ideas and concepts: self-respect, comfort, health, happiness, freedom from fear and pain.

Of course some of your prospects will be sophisticated enough to start salivating over technical drawings and statistics. They are already building powerful mental images of what they can do with this feature and you could derail their fantasy by offering your own. But the vast majority of your prospects will probably need you to throw the spotlight on the sizzle, the "what's in it for me?"

Here's an amazing contradiction: Prospects may buy your product because of a particular feature or benefit and then *never use it!* Just offering this feature makes you the kind of organization they want to do business with. Joy Johnson, Sales Manager for Loews Ventana Canyon Resort, told me how this works for her. Her job is to persuade organizations and corporations to hold their conventions and conferences at the resort. Competition is stiff and Ventana Canyon is always trying to come up with exciting new features and benefits for their clients. One that Joy thought would be especially appealing to groups with a large number of golfers was night golf, an intriguing alternative to evening receptions.

The surprising thing, says Joy, is that many groups respond positively to this suggestion and then choose another activity:

> *"They say 'I've never heard of night golf. What does it consist of?' And many groups with avid golfers think it's a great idea. But even if they*

> *don't choose to do a night golf event, the option*
> *is intriguing enough to spark their interest. It*
> *shows we can be creative with them, come up*
> *with something that perhaps no one in their*
> *group would ever do again."*

What if some of your prospects don't see a particular feature as a benefit? For example, you write down "Turn-around is 48 hours (slower than our competitor)." Should you fail to mention this fact and hope they won't notice? Probably not. The best defense is a good offense. Try to find something about this feature that could make it desirable for some prospects in some situations: "Turn-around matches your production cycle exactly—you won't have the problem of storing incoming units until you're ready to work on them." An initial drawback may even turn out to be one of your best selling points.

For example, let's say you are selling a line of shoes almost identical to your competitors' except that yours have leather soles and your competition uses a long-lasting space age synthetic that costs less and lasts three times longer. Who wants to get less for their money? Your customers, more and more, are switching to your competitors' shoes. You start by listing the feature "leather soles" and then come up with some possible benefits.

Feature: Leather soles

Benefits: Leather soles Leather "breathes" so perspiration evaporates more easily, minimizing fungus and odor. (Health, social attractiveness)

Less likely to slip on certain surfaces like vinyl or wet concrete. (Safety, freedom from pain, doctor bills, dry cleaning bills and embarrassment caused by taking a tumble on a rainy sidewalk or walking down the hall at the office.)

Leather soles are more fashionable among executives, pop stars, or any group prospects desire to associate themselves with. (Status, fashion identification.)

Leather soles don't deplete our national oil reserves. (Ecologically sound, patriotic.)

Your prospects may decide that any or all of these benefits make your shoes more valuable than similar shoes that last three times longer.

What else can you do if a particular feature is a definite drawback for some of your prospects? Here are two possibilities:

1. Find a new market.
2. Be prepared to show how the drawback is more than made up for by other benefits that your competitors don't offer. This one little weakness is what buyers must put up with to enjoy the other significant benefits of your product. Nothing is perfect.

Proceed down your list of features, brainstorming as many potential benefits as you can for each. As you start to design your presentation, think of how you can use questions to stress the perceived benefits of each feature.

When you come to tie features and benefits together in your presentation, there are two key words you should use:

"so . . . "

"because . . . "

If you start by describing a *feature*, continue with "so . . . ." Then show how that feature produces a *benefit*. If you start with the benefit, follow it with "because . . . " and mention the feature.

- This waterproofing can be sprayed on with a garden sprayer *so* it is much easier to apply and clean up.
- This waterproofing is easier to apply and clean up *because* it is made to be used with an ordinary garden sprayer.

What Motivates Your Prospects?

Try to forget everything you know about what you're selling and put yourself in your prospect's place. Write down all your positive and negative impressions. How do you perceive the service or product? Do you have a negative bias? Could you use this product or service in ways that the producer never imagined? What about the time, place, and nature of your contact with the salesperson? Write down all your positive and negative impressions.

Decide which features and benefits can be connected with your prospects' motivations. Then prepare proofs of how specific features will benefit them, solve their problem, fill their need, or fulfill their desires.

The proofs that professional salespeople offer are not always provable. Sometimes they are simply logical assumptions. Sometimes they are based on asking prospects to respect and trust the past reputation of the product or service. Remember that the purpose of any presentation is to demonstrate that your product or service will do something for your prospects that they want done. Start by understanding their desires and expectations, then match *true* benefits to *true* needs. That is the professional salesperson's simple secret for happy, loyal customers.

Do you have more than one kind of prospect? If so, should you or can you divide your prospects into more than one category, based on different needs and motivations? How many? Should you plan completely different presentations for these different categories? Or can you design interchangeable "modules" so that most of your presentation remains the same?

What questions can you ask that will appeal to your prospects' interests? If you can identify the desired benefit and motivation, then you can present from your prospects' point of view. You can establish a partnership and build trust when you get your prospects to solve their own problem by using your suggestions. When do they think they should buy? How will they make the decision? What are their procedures? Remember, you are trying to develop the partnership concept. Use questions that emphasize the WE, not the ME of the sales situation. An effective presentation is always a dialogue, not a monologue. People always defend what they have created. Let the prospect participate.

What Supports Will You Need?

What proofs and supports will you need—statistics, testimonials, lab test results, documentation, licensing, samples? (If what you're selling lends itself to third-party influence, maintain a list of contented customers and ask everybody who buys from you for a testimonial letter.) Can you show better than you can tell? Will your product or service benefit from graphic visuals—models, charts, photographs, hands-on examples? Professional salespeople know that a bit of drama adds power to even the most conservative presentation.

One way to dramatize your presentation is to plan a Show-and-Tell component to illustrate the points you want to make. The word "illustrate" makes us think of pictures, but your illustrations can appeal to all five senses: hearing, feeling, smelling, touching, and tasting.

Some professional salespeople are terrific at painting word pictures, appealing to both hearing and seeing senses. Can you demonstrate how your product performs or what the prospect will gain from using the service? Is there some way to use music in your presentation? Would the prospect respond favorably to taped messages, audio or video?

Professional salespeople know that the more involved the prospect becomes, the more chance of success the sales presentation will have. Involve as many of the senses of your prospect as possible. For example, let's suppose you're in the real estate business and you're having an open house on one of your listings. Can you arrange to have someone baking chocolate chip cookies in the kitchen? This would create an appealing odor and allow you to offer freshly baked cookies to prospective buyers. (If you lack a culinary assistant, you could simmer a pot of apples on the stove to fill the house with a homey fragrance.) Could you purchase bouquets of flowers to appeal to sense of sight? Can you hang bird feeders in the yard to attract song birds? Would the splashing of an ornamental fountain provide "white noise" to overcome the sounds of a nearby freeway? Could you prepare a fact sheet of features and benefits that prospects can read as they walk through the house? Involve all the senses.

What Objections Can You Anticipate?

Have you ever made a successful sales presentation without one question or objection from the prospect? No matter how carefully you plan your presentation, the prospect can have unanswered questions, insecurities, or natural hesitations that prevent total commitment. Sometimes this is just the prospect's need for self-expression and social exchange. Sometimes it is an unresolved concern. Either way, you must be ready to respond.

Make a list of the most common objections you've received in the past, then decide on some ways to handle them. You will answer most objections by matching your product knowledge to the prospect's motivations. The more you know about your product, the more prepared you'll be to handle common objections. Most objections are similar. They fall into four categories. What kinds do you hear most often and how will you handle them?

- Objections to your price
- Objections to your product
- Objections to your company
- Objections to you

Objections are covered in more detail in the next chapter.

Which Questions Will "Design" Your Presentation?

When you ask (and answer) enough of the right questions, your presentation can practically write itself. Start by asking yourself these "Lucky 13" questions:

1. What do I know about my prospects? What are their needs, wants, motivations?
2. What approach will I try?
3. How will I get their attention?
4. How will I build rapport?
5. What questions will I ask to establish or confirm needs?
6. What solutions can I offer for their various problems?
7. What are the specific benefits that I will stress?
8. How will I get prospects involved? What can they touch? What can they do? What can they read? What visual aids will get and keep prospects' interest?
9. Will I use third party influences? Which? Testimonial letters, names of other clients, stories, examples? How will I use them?
10. What objections might I get? How will I handle these objections? Do I have all the answers?
11. What questions will I use to confirm the benefits, to be sure that I'm understood, and to check the buying temperature?
12. What is the best sequence for my questions?
13. How will I ask for the order?

Notice that when you have answered question 12, you have created the rough outline of your presentation. Your answer to question 13 provides your closing.

What Follow-Up Can You "Build In"?

One salesperson I know worked for the Good Guys electronic chain in the San Francisco Bay Area. He asked everyone who bought another appliance, "How old is your television?" If their set was old, he'd start a conversation about the wonderful buys that Good Guys currently had on TV's. If their set was new, he'd enter their name and the age of their set in his "future sales log." This gave him immediate sales and future prospects.

Make your follow-up plan now and be prepared to make it part of your presentation. What services are you willing and able to provide after the sale? How will you satisfy your customers over and over, so when they are ready to buy again they call you? What are you willing to commit to *customer retention?* (Usually it takes a much lower energy expenditure to keep a current customer than to acquire a new one.) Chapter 9 covers the critical topic of follow-up.

STEP 3: YOUR PRESENTATION

What is the perfect sale? A man walks into a cigar shop, picks up his favorite cigar, puts down a dollar, and walks out. No one speaks. The man wants the pleasure of the cigar and the shopkeeper wants the money. The "presentation" consisted of already-established relationships: existence and location of a cigar shop, the customer's desire for a favorite cigar, agreement on price.

Your presentations will usually require more effort, but it's that simplicity that you want to strive for. Get to the point quickly, but not before you have established a rapport. You can sacrifice the perfect sale a little to build a long-term relationship with the prospect.

Pre-Contact Questions

You've planned carefully and now you're ready to make your sales contact. There's nothing more to do, right? Wrong. Take a minute to answer some pre-call questions:

- What am I doing here? What is the main objective for this sales contact?
- What benefits will this contact bring to my prospect?
- Have I done my homework? Do I know everything I can about this prospect? Do I have all the facts I need?
- Do I have a plan of action for this sales call?

- Is this person the *real* decision maker?
- What must I do to get this person to buy now?

Five Stages of Presentation

How can you be sure the prospect is involved when you give your presentation? How will you know that the prospect understands? You ask questions to progress the presentation through five stages.

1. *ATTENTION QUESTIONS.* These get favorable attention:

   - When can you give me an appointment? (not "Can you . . .")
   - How do you see yourself using this?
   - When are you going to start preparing for the old person you're going to be one day?

Get your prospect's attention and establish rapport with "me too's." If you don't have rapport immediately, start with the most recent thing you have in common with the customer. You may be saying, "I don't have *anything* in common. This is the first time I've ever seen her." But wait a minute. Perhaps you made the appointment. Or you wrote a letter or talked to her or her secretary on the phone. Or she has walked into your store or showroom of her own free will. At the very least, the two of you have ended up in the same space at the same time. *Something* happened to get you to this approach stage.

You could start by saying "Since the last time we talked, Ms. Smith . . . ." or "I see that you . . . . May I show you how this feature could work for you?"

"How would you feel if you found out a leaky roof was threatening the entire structure of your house?" That's the kind of attention-getting question that made my friend Dennis Smith one of the top salesmen for a roof restoration company, The Shake Doctors. The company is producing 300 roof restorations per month at an average of $3,300 each. He uses questions like these in both telephone and door to door solicitations to get prospects to agree to a free roof inspection: "If there's nothing wrong with the roof, we'll tell you. If there's something wrong, we'll tell you." Since few old roofs are leak-free, many prospects decide that repairs and restorations are more cost-effective than structural damage to their homes.

Confirm the connection and rapport of a previous contact or create a new, constructive one by evaluating the prospect's tastes or needs and offering her something specific. Start by establishing a connection, *any* connection. Find a common contact, but be sure it's genuine. An insincere joviality can make the friendliest prospect cringe and back off. Find something that will let you build a real bridge of rapport and identification so they say to themselves "me too" in the very first few seconds.

2. ***INTEREST QUESTIONS.*** These stimulate interest:

- Is this big enough for your needs?
- How would you like to drive a new BMW for the weekend?
- This plan saved your competitor $10,000 in the first year. Would you like me to figure what *your* savings would be?

You've got your prospects' attention. Now you build their interest. Take your list of features and benefits and make intriguing comments about them to hold your customer's interest. Start searching for the motivations that will make your product indispensable to your prospect.

Sally Henderson, director of Convention Sales for the San Francisco Convention and Tourist Bureau, has a dynamite interest- raising question:

> *Most big organizations use their conferences as profit- makers to fund other services they give their members. So when I'm promoting citywide conventions, I know increasing their attendance is a prime motivator. First, I always ask about how many people they project will come.*

> *When they give me a number, I ask my second question: 'How would you like to have the largest attendance you've ever had at a convention?'*
>
> *Then I ask if they realize that, in addition to all their activities and speakers, San Francisco itself is a big drawing card? Do they know that it is one of the most popular cities to visit in the world? I ask them if they've ever ridden our "cable cars that go halfway to the stars?" Are they familiar with our extraordinary views, the Golden Gate Bridge, Fisherman's Wharf, Union Square, and the other things that make San Francisco unique? Are they aware that they can walk to most attractions because San Francisco is a compact city? Do they know that San Francisco is literally the city with something for everyone? And that when a convention is held in San Francisco, it almost always has a record attendance?*

Create identification with you and your product. That means that you answer their unspoken questions about "What's it going to do for me?" and "So what?" You want them saying, "Hey, me too! I could use that."

3. **CONVICTION QUESTIONS.** These prove need:

- What's the worst thing that could happen to you?
- How competitive does your company want to be?
- What other models have you looked at? How close did they come to satisfying your needs?
- Is this what you had in mind?

Ask fact-finding questions that will confirm or disprove what you think you already know about the customer. In your pre-call planning you did your homework, so you know why you are there. You believe you're talking to a prospect. The fact-finding questions will help you validate the information you've collected and add new things that you just couldn't have found out before you were face to face.

George Nicholson has developed a questioning concept that is famous within the industry. He is vice president of marketing and sales for Software Solutions in Atlanta. One of their software systems manages wholesale warehouse operations and sells for between $20,000 and $80,000. George's salespeople approach prospects and ask something like: "Do you ever wonder why some companies grow and succeed while others die?" They listen carefully to the customer's reply, then incorporate it in a question like: "Do you think that companies with good management succeed, while companies with poor management almost always fail?" Or they ask, "Have you ever watched a company fail? Do you think it was because of poor management?" They go on to suggest that "luck" is "preparation meeting opportunity." With the Software Solutions' warehouse management system, the prospects will be in the perfect position to "get lucky." This question approach has generated more than $30 million in yearly sales through dealers.

4. **DESIRE QUESTIONS.** These arouse desire with benefits:

- Which model is your favorite?
- If you could buy two instead of one, which would the second one be?
- How much money (or time) will this save you?

All potential customers have a "hot button," an emotional trigger that makes them want to act. By asking questions based on the benefits of your product, you will discover what excites and motivates your prospect. Build on this to create desire, to "raise the buying temperature."

Carol Kuhn, the enterprising woman who had customers diving for her Lady Remington Fashion Jewelry, is adept that this:

Nine times out of ten, people come to my presentations thinking they are just going to buy a pair of earrings, but usually go home with much more than they planned. I show them different ways to make ensembles and ask 'Do you want this in silver or gold?' Often they take both and the sale builds and builds. Once I asked my standard opening question, 'What are you looking for?' and the woman replied 'Everything! My house was just robbed.' Before you knew it we piled up a whole tray of jewelry and she bought it all.

5. **ACTION QUESTIONS.** These prompt decision to buy:

- What do *we* need to do to convince the boss?
- What kind of support service do you want to have from us?
- Shall I check the delivery schedule on that?

These are closing questions. Sometimes they are a trial close to show you how far along the road you have come. Often they are the final question to complete the agreement. All are designed to get a reaction from the prospect. All require a decision. Be sure your prospect is ready to receive an action question, then fire away.

Ed Ayd of Dataserv says, "Your customers understand the way their companies work better than you do. Get them to help you close: 'What is the next step in the process?' 'What do we need to do to get this thing done?' When a customer starts talking about 'us' instead of 'you,' it means you are beginning to be a team."

Four Questions You Should Be Ready to Answer

You've built empathy by asking questions, and you have the information you need to start your presentation. Now it's your turn to answer the customer's questions. Here are some typical questions that the customer may ask:

1. "What's in it for me?" (WIFM) From your initial questions, you've already decided which features and benefits will best meet the customer's needs.
2. "Who else has used this?" Have testimonials ready, either copies of letters or a list of references they can call. You could also have a prepared handout with facts and figures on the success of your product or service.
3. "What benefits did your other customers get?" Prospects want to be able to say "me too." Few people like being *too* different. They like to take risks and experiment, but they also want the tried and tested. Show them how others have benefit with your product.
4. "Who says that you can deliver?" That means sell yourself and your company's reputation for timeliness, quality and service.

Review these points before going into your presentation. You might want to write them down and look at them before you meet with your prospect.

The Seven Questions Prospects Must Ask You

Be prepared to answer seven key questions before prospects buy from you. Prospects can ask these questions in any order. They may already have asked themselves some of these questions and then supplied their own answers before your contact. What are these questions?

1. "Will I talk to this salesperson?" To get the interview you must create curiosity. Pose a question about a benefit or a feature that makes the customer say, "I'd like to talk to this person." Sometimes this is accomplished with an advertisement or letter before you see them.
2. "Will I listen to this salesperson?" To get prospects to listen to you, *you* must listen to them. Get their attention by listening to their questions and responding with your own. In a store or showroom, this usually starts with "How can I help you?"
3. "Do I need this?" Make sure prospects recognize and understand their own needs, then reveal how you can fill

them. "How would you use this?" —"What kind of speed do you need?"—"Will this save you money?"

4. "Does the product really give me these benefits?" Reconfirm the benefits, offer proofs, and get the prospects to agree that they are valid. Restate the prospect's buying motives and then tie them to the features and benefits.

5. "Is this the best source for this product or service?" Create positive opinions about the service, convenience, and reliability of your company and you. Establish confidence, trust, and acceptance. Will your prospects act? Even if your product satisfies all of their needs or wants, and even if they agree with every major point you make, some people are simply afraid to make a decision. Design your presentation so that the decision to buy is almost automatic. What can you do to be sure that when it's time to commit, your prospects will act?

6. "Is the price reasonable?" You shouldn't be asking "Is the price affordable?" when your involved in your presentation. That's part of your qualifying stage. By this time you should already have established that prospects can *afford* the price. Now you want your prospects to *accept* the price. Show how the price is fair for the advantages the prospects will receive. Perhaps it's not the lowest price attainable, but it's worth the price you're asking. Repeat the benefits, if necessary, to show that the pain of giving up the money is offset by the pleasure of satisfying the need.

7. "Should I buy (now)?" This is the final question in the sale. Demonstrate the advantages and pleasures that will begin when the purchase is made. Contrast them with the drawbacks of missed potential. The "now" part of the question is always implied, even though the prospect may not say it. Remember that a strong buying motive is fear of loss. Emphasize how loss can be avoided by buying *now*. The prospect can avoid loss by at least beginning the buying process, the ordering, financing, etc. (Of course if there is a good reason for delaying the purchase—too early in the growth of the company, wrong method for current set-up,

changing market conditions—you will agree that it is wise to wait. Provide an interim solution to the prospect's problem, and arrange to be there when the prospect reaches the next stage.)

Learn to recognize these seven questions, spoken or implied, so you're prepared to respond without effort or distraction. Learn also to recognize when prospects have already answered these questions in their own minds. Ask questions that get the prospect to confirm each decision so you are sure they accept their own judgment.

How Do You End Your Sales Contact?

Every sales contact should end on a positive note. This profoundly affects your future relationship with your prospects and how you feel about yourself as a professional salesperson. Do you say a cheerful "Good bye," "so long," or "see you next month" and shake hands? Or does your conversation just sort of peter out and you slink away as your prospect is distracted by ringing phones or an associate's interruption?

Even on the telephone, end on a strong note. I have an otherwise-delightful friend who simply hangs up when she's said what she wants to say. It's very disconcerting and makes me feel I'm not important to her. What if you really have to end a conversation quickly? Hank Tristler, the real estate sales trainer, suggests: "If you don't wish to continue the conversation, wait until you're talking and hang up in the middle of a sentence. They'll never believe you hung up on yourself." That's funny, but it's also true! The other person believes a mechanical malfunction ended the conversation, rather than your lack of interest. But I recommend this only for emergencies. It's much better to end on a positive note.

Never end a sales contact by saying:

- I guess I won't keep you any longer.
- Well, I'll let you get back to work.
- I should be going.

If you have to apologize for talking to a prospect or for being there, then something is wrong with the whole exchange. Don't tag a negative end onto a positive conversation. Be sure that you have good reason to be there and that you're proud of what you're doing. Then end your conversation with:

"Thank you. It's been nice talking with you."

Conduct and end your conversations in a positive manner. If the other person feels good and you feel good, the next contact will start on a positive note.

Should You Memorize Your Presentation?

Don't memorize your entire presentation, just the *outline*. Then fill in the supporting information in your own words as you go. This produces a "planned, not canned" presentation.

How do you remember all those things without mixing them up or forgetting an important point? The simplest way is a "peg system" that goes back thousands of years. It's call "mnemonics" after the Greek goddess of memory, Mnemosyne. Ancient orators like Plato and Socrates remembered the key points of their lengthy speeches by "pegging" each key point to another structure that they already knew well. For example, they could use parts of the body starting at the head and going down, or the rooms of their house starting at the front door.

If you have five points you want to be sure to make, you might match each to a finger of your left hand and tick them off as you go. Three points could be head - body - legs and you could "mark" your place inconspicuously with your left hand. You can remember as many as twenty points easily by dividing them into four five-item units:

- HEAD: hair, forehead, eyes, nose, mouth
- BODY: chest, waist, hips, knees, feet

- HOME: hallway, living room, dining room, kitchen, pantry
- OFFICE: (starting from door and working clockwise around room) copy machine, coffee machine, window, desk, filing cabinet

One excellent book on how to use this memory technique is *Total Recall: How to Boost Your Memory Power* by Joan Minninger, Ph.D. The advantages of having a fixed framework and then improvising the details are:

- The customer can't throw you off track. When they interrupt, ask a question, or have an objection, you handle it and then go right back to your outline. Of course you're smart enough to decide when to drop a segment or reverse the sequence. (Easy to do with the mnemonic techniques described above—just reverse.)
- You're relaxed and confident. You know what you are going to say. You can pay closer attention to your prospects and what they are saying since you don't have to concentrate on the order of the sales points.

How Do You Communicate Your Message?

The best definition of communication I have ever heard is "fostering understanding." Speaking and listening skills make up an important part of communication, but to understand and to be understood, that is real communication.

For example, what did you have for breakfast this morning? Was it the upper part of a hog's hind leg with two bird embryos? Or ham and eggs? Both may be correct (unless you're watching your cholesterol), but each conveys the same information in a different way.

Say what you mean, and mean what you say. We often say things we don't mean, and we mean things we don't say. Then we wonder why people don't respond the way we expected. Maybe we are not really communicating, not *fostering understanding.*

One study suggests that in normal speech people communicate just 7 percent of their feelings and attitudes with words. Thirty-eight percent are communicated by tone of voice and 55 percent by non-verbal signals. So communication is more than words. It's also the tone of your words and your body language.

Communicating with Words

Here are some interesting facts about words. Did you know that there are 3,700 languages and dialects in our world? That there are over 650,000 words in the English language? That the average college graduate recognizes about 30,000 words? That Shakespeare used 36,000 different words, but the King James Bible only 8,000. And that the average person uses only about 5,000 words and can hold a fairly lengthy conversation with only 200? We use the same words over and over many times during the day.

To be successful in sales, get the maximum effect out of your words. Many psychologists agree that certain words have an emotional impact no matter how they are used. Communication experts have tried to identify these "power" words. When you look at the lists they've come up with, you realize that professional salespeople's talk is already loaded with these words. We call them the "sales vocabulary." For example:

- Expressive words: luxurious, fool-proof, delectable, flawless
- Dynamic words: break-through, rugged, power, speed
- Personal words: you, me, I, we, our, your.

What kinds of words are appropriate to your presentation? How many can you think of? Get out your dictionary and thesaurus and list as many words as you can that will help you convey meaning and emotion. How many can you tie to your product or service? Table 1 shows very powerful words. It's just a sample. Tie your product to power words throughout the alphabet. Soon you'll have a sales vocabulary second to none—won't you?

Years ago, one of my dear friends in selling tried to find a new way to describe his product every day, using words that he had never used before. It wasn't easy, but soon he had a dozen ways to explain his product without repeating himself. This let him adapt his presentation to the knowledge and personal experience of almost any prospect.

Can you increase your vocabulary, but stick to straightforward language? Eschew obfuscation? Avoid buzz words, industry words, or any slang that may confuse your prospect? Some industries have their own languages that baffle outsiders. Recently a computer consultant sent me a bill saying he had "investigated the source of connectivity problems between systems, ordered upgrades, and discovered errors arising out of difficulties of nonstandard disk partitioning and faulty on-site back-ups." It's okay to talk like that if you're sure your prospect does too. If not, stick to nontechnical explanations. Speak your prospect's language.

Communicating with Tone

A successful sales presentation requires more than words alone. Learn to use the right tone, inflection and phrasing.

Tape your own voice and listen. Most of us don't recognize our own voices when we hear them. What mental picture do you make of the person speaking on the tape? Do you hear the qualities in your voice that you were trying to project? Would you like to listen to this voice for a half hour or more? Or would it become grating, boring, irritating? Do you need to lower the pitch? Slow down? Speed up? Reduce or increase the animation?

One of the most common vocal problems is a voice that slides into an unpleasant upper register when the speaker is excited. The voice becomes tight and thin, tiring to listen to and tiring to the speaker as well. Does this ever happen to you? If so, try this exercise. Stand up straight, relax your neck and throat, open your mouth and say slowly: "Ding dong, King Kong, ping pong."

Table 1

ability	credible	harmonious
abundant	definite	health
achieve	dependable	home
active	deserving	honesty
admirable	desirable	honor
advantage	determined	hospitality
advance	distinction	humor
affluence	diversity	imagination
affordable	durable	improvement
amusement	ease	independent
affection	economy	industry
ambition	effective	ingenuity
appreciate	efficient	initiative
appetite	elegance	integrity
approval	energy	intelligence
appetite	enhance	judgment
approval	enormous	low-cost
aspire	enthusiasm	love
authoritative	equality	modern
bargain	excel	money
beauty	excellence	mother
benefit	exceptional	motivation
capable	exclusive	necessary
cheer	expedite	patriotism
civic pride	expressive	personality
children	faith	popularity
clean	fidelity	practical
comfort	fitting	praiseworthy
commendable	fun	prestige
comprehensive	future	proficient
concentration	genuine	progress
onfidence	good	prominent
conscientious	grateful	propriety
cooperation	growth	prosperous
courage	guarantee	punctual
courtesy	handsome	quality

reasonable	stablility	truth
recognition	status	universal
recommend	stimulating	useful
reliable	stylish	utility
relief	substantial	valuable
reputable	success	vigor
responsible	superior	vital
safe	supreme	vivid
salient	sympathy	wisdom
satisfactory	tasteful	you
scientific	tested	yours
service	thinking	youth
simplicity	thorough	zeal
sincerity	thrift	zenith
sociable	time-saving	zesty
sports	trustworthy	

Repeat the phrase five more times, dropping your voice to a slightly lower tone each time. This will help pull your words down into your throat where the sound is deeper and has more resonance. Right or wrong, many people consider lower voices more authoritative. If you repeat this exercise several times a day, you will develop a mellower, more controlled speaking voice.

More important than just the tone is the emotion behind the voice. Put alertness and interest in your voice. Build a warm, pleasant, personal voice image. Smile, even if—especially if—you are talking to your prospect on the telephone. Did you know you can hear a smile?

Try to develop a distinctive voice. Speak clearly and distinctly. Move your lips. Move your tongue. Move your jaw. Talk directly to the person. If it's on the phone, talk directly into the mouthpiece. A well-modulated voice carries, so use a normal tone of voice. Talk at a moderate rate. Vary your tone. It will emphasize your meaning and add color and vitality to what you have to say.

Communicating with Body Language

You've prepared your presentation carefully, your words are well chosen, and your voice is bright and friendly. What is your body language saying about you?

Practice giving your presentation to yourself in a mirror. If possible, could you set up a video camera and tape some practice and real presentations? Observe the stranger that is you. Do you have any unconscious nervous mannerisms that signal unease? Ear pulling, hair twirling, tie straightening, hem pulling, nose scratching, talking with your hand over your mouth, rocking your chair so it balances on the two back legs, leaning so close that prospects back away, foot shuffling, lip smacking, thigh slapping, shrugging, or grimacing? If they bother you on the tape, imagine how they will affect your prospects in person. Work on eliminating them.

This *doesn't* mean that you want to be totally free of any expressiveness. The greatest communicators all have their own unique gestures and expressions. Develop the mannerisms that feel right for you, that express you positively, and that bring a positive reaction from your prospects. Eliminate the twitches and glitches that convey nothing but nervousness and doubt.

Communicating by Doing

Ultimately you communicate by what you do. Live the part. Look the part. Be the part. Be the service-oriented, caring, advisory, modern professional salesperson. Example is always better than explanation. We can explain and explain and explain, but unless our actions are in harmony, our explanations are useless.

Doing increases your personal self-esteem. If you make a promise, no matter how small it is, and you keep it, you feel good about yourself. Your confidence increases. But if you make a promise and you break it, you lose self-esteem. You don't feel as good.

Paula Ebejer knows about going the extra mile for her clients. She is territory manager for a food broker, Bradshaw North. Food salespeople know that their equivalent of the Emmy and Oscar is getting their product an end-of-aisle display in any big supermarket. Her clients included the legendary Marina Safeway in San Francisco, immortalized in fact and fiction as one of the best places for young professionals to meet each other as well as the largest dollar-grossing store in northern California.

If the manager asked anything, had any kind of problem, I followed through. I was always asking about what was coming up in the way of a promotion or a contest. I'd try to anticipate his needs. For Chinese New Year, he was doing an "end" with one of our Chinese dinner products. I went to Chinatown and got them a lot of Chinese lanterns and decorations. He won an award from Safeway for the display. I always tried to come through for them.

Recently they really came through for me. A major manufacturer was in San Francisco for a convention. We wanted to have every market in the city looking good for them, but especially the Marina Safeway because there was a huge event across the street on the Marina Green for 2,000 of their people and the general public. The whole Marina Safeway came through for me. The man who builds the "ends" built three ends in a row of featuring our products. The same man was going to be on vacation but he

> brought in enough product to keep the ends
> stocked while he was off.
>   When you walked in the store, you saw the
> freezer case full of our ice cream with the candy
> above it and then huge ends of our candy, rice,
> and pet food. They kept filling them up. I was
> amazed that he would do all that for us. I went
> to thank him and he said, "I felt this was really
> important for you from the way you talked."

When Paula kept her promises to her clients, she gained both her own self-esteem and their loyalty. They came through for her the same way she had always come through for them. So make promises to your client, to yourself, to your company, to your industry, to your community, to your family. Then be sure that every promise you make, you keep. Always do what makes you proud. Never do what diminishes you, what makes you ashamed. Speak, listen, and do. Those are the secrets of successful sales communication.

Eight Questions to Improve Your Presentation Skills

As you polish your presentation skills, ask yourself these eight questions.

1. How do I greet people, both in person and on the telephone? There is nothing worse than picking up a phone and hearing a flat, dead voice on the other end. Do you extend your hand when you meet someone? Do you smile? Do you say "Happy to meet you" ? Do you greet them with a positive first thought? Do you use words that trigger their emotions?
2. Does my face know how I feel? I've met people who don't let their faces show how they feel. They may be excited, but you'd never guess it. Let your face express your feel-

ings. Even when you feel lousy, adjust your attitude and put on the best face you can.

3. Do I interrupt? I must admit that it took a great effort to break my habit of interrupting the other person. In fact, I'm not sure I'm entirely over it in my personal life. But I have conquered interrupting in my business life because I know that if I interrupt I may very well lose the sale. This is a hard habit to break, but it's one you need to work on constantly.

4. Do I speak clearly and slowly? People often can't listen as fast as you can talk. Stop, pause and give them a chance to absorb what you are saying. Ask if they understand. If not, restate for clarification.

5. What about the tone and pitch of my voice? Is it pleasant? Enthusiasm makes some salespeople talk faster, louder, or higher. The more excited they get, the harder they are to understand. I've noticed on television recently that contemporary actors try to show emotion by becoming louder, higher, and faster. Shouting can capture attention, but as a long-term communication tool it is useless. People understand and accept more when listening is a pleasant experience.

6. Do I exaggerate? The modern, sensitive, and service-oriented salesperson can't afford to. Sell, don't oversell. Just tell the truth about your product and your company. It's amazing how useful truth can be in communicating what you want people to know. The professional salesperson is selling a philosophy as well as a product. People need to believe in your honesty and integrity. Rudy Duban, a great salesman who trained me in my early years, used to tell me that it is easy to seem sincere and truthful if you are sincere and truthful. George Burns said, "Sincerity is the secret of success. Once you can fake that, you've got it made." As funny as that line is, don't fake it. Be real.

7. Am I good at remembering names? Psychologists tell us that the word we most love to hear and see is our own name! Develop a system for remembering the names of

all your prospects and customers. Repeat it, write it down, read it over and over to yourself until it's locked in your mind. If you still have a problem, try some of the systems in the various books on memory techniques. For example, try to associate the name with an object or famous person, make a rhyme out of it, or construct an anagram.

8. Do my sales contacts end on a positive note? Ending a sales contact requires the same sense of rhythm and awareness that a dancer uses to end an impromptu performance on a high note. Are you aware of the signals you are getting from your prospect so you know when and how to go for the "ta- DAH!"?

Ten Questions to Rate Your Presentation

You're out in the hall, back in your office, or sitting at home in the evening. Take the time to evaluate the sales contacts you made during the day, mentally at least if not on a sheet of paper that you file for future reference.

1. Did I involve the customer?
2. Did I ask the right questions?
3. Did I give examples?
4. Did I ask about and address the prospect's needs?
5. Did I help the prospect find a solution?
6. Did I offer proofs?
7. Did I use showmanship?
8. Did I demonstrate the product?
9. Did I use questions to confirm understanding and acceptance?
10. Did I ask for the order?

The Greek philosopher Aristotle divided human response into ethos, pathos, and logos. Ethos means to make a connection with another party, to establish empathy. Pathos is to appeal to the feelings and emotions. Logos is logic. All three must be present in an effective presentation.

A good presentation requires solid preparation, inspiration, hard work, experiment, and constant rethinking. It smoothly combines the complex elements of a space launch, a Broadway show, or a gourmet dinner. And the thrill of success is just as big.

"Questions can uncover information that your prospect isn't aware of yet, develop ideas that haven't really been thought out. They can help you spot a dissatisfaction or show you a way you can do something better. When you ask interesting questions that provoke thought on their part—even if you're irritating your prospect at first— if you hit the right question and get them talking to you, then you've got them in your court and the longer you keep them there, the better chance you have to make the sale."

Kelly Gutierrez
Organizational Sales
Representative
Knott's Berry Farm

7

Objection Questions

"Which means more to you—a batch of M.B.A. degrees? Or solid experience, maturity, and judgment?"
Beat out two large, prestigious firms for a lucrative consultant contract. (See page 129.)

"You feel our price is too high? Can you be more specific?"
Sold 20,000 picnics. (See page 131.)

"If you had a bad steak in a restaurant, would you stop eating steak?"
Gets 70 percent of prospects to drop objection and listen. (See page 137.)

W e had made half a dozen successful sales calls during the morning, but at lunch the young trainee who was accompanying me sat staring gloomily at his hamburger. "Not enough onions?" I asked.

"No, not enough objections!"

He'd been taught that handling objections was the key to selling, so he'd looked forward to watching how a "pro" handled them. There was just one problem: no objections. I've almost never had any objections in my selling career because I try to anticipate and meet them in my presentation, before they become a point of resistance.

The professional salesperson knows that the best way to handle objections is not to have any. If you've asked the right qualifying, probing, and presentation questions, you'll rarely run into objections.

The next best way is to treat objections as an opportunity for further probing. When objections do come up, they can usually be turned into selling advantages. The worst prospects are those who sit back, listen attentively to your story, and nod pleasantly. Do they understand what you are saying? Are you addressing their needs? Should you even go on with the presentation? Without objections—whether you overcome them in advance with your presentation or on the spot with your questioning skills—there would be no need for a salesperson. A vending machine could do the job just as well.

It's true that objections can be valuable keys to your prospect's needs and wants, but they are not always the unmixed blessing that some would like you to think. Sometimes "It's too expensive; It's not good enough; I'm not interested" actually mean that it's too expensive, it's not good enough, and the prospect is definitely not interested. You simply didn't qualify sufficiently.

How to Respond to Objections

Objections are often called ladders, sign posts, or handles to getting the sale. A more useful image might be to think of an objection as a ball that the prospect has lobbed into your court. You can sizzle the ball back to the other side (by listing lots of features and benefits) so the prospect is left to recover from this assault, focusing on internal self-talk while you rush on with your presentation. OR you can involve the prospect in pursing the answer with you. That means asking questions.

Convert objections into questions. Restate them and have the prospects restate them. This is an opportunity for prospects to rethink and clarify their thoughts. Do this as many times as necessary. Keep restating their objections until you are absolutely sure that both of you understand them.

Probing Objections

The most valuable way to think of objections is that they are another form of probing. Here's an example.

Prospect: We just replaced all the equipment in this department a year ago. It took my staff nine months to learn how to use the new system. I'm not going through all that trouble and expense again just to prevent a few returns. (objection)

You: Oh, are you getting returns? About how many? (probing questions)

Prospect: A few, but not enough to make it worth buying new equipment!

You: This new model could drop your reject rate to less than .04 percent. That should make your customers happy and save you money. (benefits)

Prospect: I can think of a lot of ways to keep our customers happy that would cost a heck of a lot less! (rejection)

Let's back up to that first objection and see what skilled questioning might do.

Prospect: We just replaced all the equipment in this department a year ago. It took my staff nine months to learn how to use the new system. I'm not going through all that trouble and expense again just to save a few returns.

You: Oh, are you getting returns? About how many?

Prospect: A few, but not enough to make it worth buying new equipment!

You: You say "a few" returns. How do you handle them?

And with more questions you try to lead your prospect to analyze what returns are really costing the company and how your product will offer more benefits and fewer problems than sticking with the system he's got. Listen carefully to the answer to each question and use it to frame the next one! Some possibilities are:

- Do you give a straight refund on returns or ship them replacements?
- Who receives the returns? Who checks out the defective parts to confirm the problem? Who ships the replacement? Who handles the paperwork? Does any of this ever cause overtime?
- How does your bookkeeping department handle the exchange? How long does that take them? Do you ever have a problem carrying over outstanding credits for returns? Do you ever offer clients a discount or free replacements to keep them happy?
- Do you personally follow up with the clients who return defective parts? How often do you have to do that? Do you supervise the people responsible for handling the returns? How much time does all this take?
- Have you ever had a client threaten legal action because a part malfunctioned?
- Do returns affect your insurance rate?

By this time both you and the prospect are probably starting to have a different idea about what defective parts are costing the company. This is where you make some notes so you can suggest or work out a dollar figure to the prospect: "So currently returns are costing you about $00,000 and 000 hours annually . . . ."

- So if you got your return rate close to zero, and if you personally saved about four hours a week, and if you could do both of those things for less than what it's costing you now, you'd consider a change? Right?

But what if it becomes obvious after a question or two that returns really aren't a problem or, perhaps more important, that the prospect absolutely refuses to see them as a problem? The instant you realize this—from the prospect's answers and body language— stop immediately and go on to another area. Remember that the prospect was unhappy about how long it took people to learn to use the new system?

Prospect: It took my staff nine months to learn how to use the new system. I'm not going through all that trouble again.

That's your next clue. Go for it!

- What made your new system so hard to learn?
- You say it's too complicated. Can you give me an example?
- Do you think your staff had a special reason for resisting the change?
- What kind of instructions did your people get?
- Did you have professional training? In-house? Outside classes? What problems did you run into?
- Are the same employees still with your company? What affect has your new equipment had on your turn-over rate? Positive or negative? Why do you think that is?

All this time you're gathering new information about the prospect's problems. Again, if training isn't seen as the problem, stop and go on. Coax the prospect into analyzing the problem. Is the equipment too sophisticated for the available work force? Are employee incentives to learn a new system too low? Are other working conditions at fault? Are there issues unrelated to the system that have affected productivity or error rate?

Listen to the words and watch any body signals for clues that you're on the wrong track—the prospect has crossed arms, leans back in the chair in a non-committed pose, or keeps looking around the room. Even if the real problem is immediately clear to you, *never* keep hammering away with your prepared probing/objection questions if the prospect grows uncomfortable or bored. The prospect will either pretend to agree with you to get you out the door without a fuss and without the sale, or the prospect will personally offer to show you the door.

So listen. Accept. Continue.

"Why Should I Buy from You?"

When Ron Von Trapp was with Exxon, they were trying to persuade a Japanese forklift company in San Francisco to switch from IBM to Exxon typewriters. The company's president was in town and sat in on the presentation. We had covered the benefits in detail.

> *Their president—a very formal dignified man— was sitting next to me. After we had finished the presentation and our sales manager asked for the order, the president turned to me. In carefully phrased English, he asked, "Mr. Trapp, would you please tell me why my company should buy typewriters from you instead of from IBM?"*
>
> *"Sir," I said, "with all due respect, would you please tell me why my company should buy one of your forklifts instead of your competitor's?" The president started to answer me. Then he stopped and said: "Very well done." We got the order.*

Seven Ways to Respond to Objections

Even the best-prepared presentation is bound to be met with an objection at some point. How do you handle one? Here are seven tips.

1. Rehearse. Being sensitive to the prospect doesn't mean you don't have to plan responses to objections. Do your basic homework. Then use skilled probing questions to reveal features and benefits whenever possible.

2. Listen attentively to the entire objection. Don't jump in with a response as soon as the first idea is presented. When prospects hear themselves talk, their objections may sound less and less important or valid. Wait until there is total silence. (And sometimes wait a few beats longer. The prospect may try to end the brief pause by amplifying the objection or even by resolving it: "But, then, it's not really that important . . . .") It's absolutely human to want to jump in with "But my widget is better," or "I can tell you how that works." Don't. Let the prospect get it all out. The best listener is the best salesperson.

3. Agree. Never challenge. Never, *never* make prospects defend their objections. This locks them into an adversarial position. The worst word a salesperson can start a sentence with is "but." Never argue, not about price, not about what anyone said, not about anything. Agree, then lead them on.

- I'm sorry I didn't make that clear. Would you like to see me demonstrate that again?
- You're sharp to pick up on that! Usually that's absolutely correct. However, with this feature (or financing plan or guarantee) . . . . Is that one of your priorities?
- I can see why you figure it that way, and lots of our current customers started out like that too. Would you like me to try to arrange for you to talk to one of our best customers who . . . ?
- That shows you're really on top of the budget in your department, so . . . . How would a benefit like that work with your current program?

If saying "I'm sorry that . . . " is hard for you, practice! Don't protect your own self-esteem or display your dazzling expertise by making a prospect feel stupid. You may win ego points but you'll lose a customer.

4. Lead, don't push. (Remember my seminar demonstration, described in Chapter 1, on how people respond to resistance: they resist it!)

5. Convert all objections into questions. Questions invite answers. Objections invite arguments. The prospect says "Your program won't work for me."

Don't say: "Sure it will."

Say: "You raise a good point. How exactly could this program integrate with your present system? What do you need to know or do to make it work?

6. Respond immediately to each objection, even if you have to cover points you planned to use in your closing. For example, if a price objection occurs early in your presentation, ask: "Does that seem like a lot of money? Maybe this won't turn out to be the right program for you. Shall we stop and figure the actual cost so we can see how much money these features are going to save you?" If you don't respond to each objection immediately, you'll lose your prospects' attention. They'll be thinking about the objection and why you haven't responded to it, so they'll stop participating in the sales process.

   Handle the objection at once. If you can't, write it down. Yes, I mean take a piece of paper, have it in front of you, and write down the objection. If it is absolutely impossible to answer the objection at once, you might say, "An excellent point, Ms. Freeman! Let me write that down so I can respond to it when we go over the installation process." I have never yet had anyone say, "No, Answer it now." Prospects know you are taking them seriously when their comment is important enough for you to write it down and come back to it.

7. Discover the real objections through skillful questioning. "Too expensive" usually means "interest is too low." When you think you've found the real objection, help the

prospect discover the real and perceived benefits of your product through more questioning.

Five Major Causes of Objections

Most objections can be narrowed down to one or a combination of five causes:

1. Insufficient qualifying: The prospect doesn't need or want what you are offering. (If this is the case, none of the other causes matter.)
2. Insufficient probing: You have failed to determine the prospect's true feelings, opinions, and needs. (Improve your probing skills.)
3. Unclear presentation: The prospect is confused, misinterprets your explanation, or doesn't get enough information about your product or service to make a proper decision. (Improve your presentation skills.)
4. Undeveloped listening and response skills: You ignore or do not put enough significance on the points that the prospect feels are important. (Practice listening and responding appropriately.)
5. Undeveloped personal image: The prospect doesn't respect your knowledge, doesn't trust your integrity, isn't sure you'll be able to provide ongoing support during a long-term buyer- seller relationship. (Improve your product knowledge and work harder on your listening and response skills.)

Little Guys versus Big Guys

One day Alice Bullwinkle, a financial consultant in Denver, got a call from a very successful and wealthy prospect. The woman asked if Alice wanted to bid for her account. Alice's competition would be the two biggest financial planning firms in Denver.

The prospect asked her a test question: "What would you say if you were asked to make a speech at a graduation?"

Alice's answer obviously pleased her for she continued: "What should be the woman's perspective on financial planning?" Again Alice "passed" the test. Then Alice had a question of her own: "You're considering these two other firms and they're very proud of the M.B.A.s on their staffs. Their recruiting method is to find outstanding students and put them on staff as planners. But, what is the role of judgment, maturity and experience in the planning process?" Then Alice described her own years of experience. The prospect chose Alice and became one of her largest clients.

Five Types of Objections

The objections you will run into are usually one of five basic types.

The Product Objection

Did you verify the prospect's needs? Buyers will not object to a product they feel will help them accomplish their objectives. Are you sure the prospect agrees that this is the best product solution? How do you handle a product or service objection? To begin with, don't panic. Restate the objection, then ask questions that reveal the feelings and opinions of the prospect while you get the objection out in the open. Go back and stress the benefits backed by the features. Explain the service you will provide compared to your competitor or predecessor. Most product or service objections grow out of unpleasant past experiences. Be sure that you are identifying your prospects' feelings. Ask an open-ended question to be sure you have the true objection out in the open. "What else is important?" "What did you do when that happened?" "How does your department staff (or colleagues or CEO) feel about that?" You cannot handle an objection if you do not know what it is.

The Company Objection

Prospects may lack confidence that the company will deliver all you say it will. Establish the reputation of the company

early. Stress the strong points—for example; years in business, philosophy, other satisfied customers, and past suc-
cesses. Be sure your prospect agrees that your company is
one they want to do business with.

The Price Objection

One of the most common objections for many products and
services is price. Are you prepared to prove that value is
different from price? Price is what the buyer pays. Value is
what the buyer gets. Your question should be, *what does the
prospect feel is valuable about my product or service?*
    To overcome a price objection:

- Be sure you are selling value.
- Be sure the prospect *sees* the value.

Whenever you hear a price objection, take a deep breath
and restate the objection as a question: "You think it will cost
more to install this new valve than it will save you?" Then
resell the product. Resell the features and benefits until the
prospect sees the value as greater than the cost.
    Use questions like: "So the price is your only problem,
right?" If you, the professional salesperson, can isolate a single objection, you can usually overcome it: "If I show you
how you could afford to have what we are offering, would
that solve your problem?" Again, isolate the objection. Make
the value you are offering more important than the money
objection. Everything costs something, but value is relative. A
$10 can of soda might not sell in a supermarket, but it would
probably be a hit in the middle of a desert or as the cheapest
beverage at a chic nightclub. When the perceived benefits
outweigh the price, the prospect will buy.
    Kelly Gutierrez is organizational sales rep for Knott's Berry
Farm in southern California. She persuades organizations to
hold their events at the "park" as they call it. Because Knott's
provides a top-quality package, price can be a concern.

*If they say we're too expensive and they've
chosen a cheaper site, I ask them if we can*

*compare our costs with those in our competitor's
proposals: 'You feel our price is too high? Can
you be more specific? Are you clear on the cost
breakout?' When we go through the proposals
together, we always find that Knott's price includes many items that our competitors have left
out, so the cost differential is much, much
smaller. Some of our competitors tend to leave
out essential costs like taxes and gratuities when
they send their proposals. We don't.*

Recently Kelly was courting a large insurance company
that holds an annual picnic. The corporate planner was stuck
with a budget that seemed to rule out Knott's Berry Farm.
Kelly asked if she could have permission to go to the CEO: "I
don't believe in going past anyone if it makes them uncomfortable—otherwise they can shoot you down." She contacted the CEO who hadn't even known that Knott's
produced corporate picnics. She told him about all the company events that Knott's has handled and persuaded the CEO
that Knott's price was competitive because it included everything. "Can you imagine what taxes and tips for 10,000 people
would add to a lower bid that hadn't included them?"

Kelly persuaded the CEO to increase the budget for their
event. Soon 10,000 insurance company employees and their
families were having a terrific picnic at the park. "They must
have enjoyed it," says Kelly, "because they've been back a
second time."

The Personal Objection

This one is tough. Sometimes personalities don't mix. If you
suspect that prospects aren't buying you, face it directly. Ask
if they have any problem dealing with you personally.

Is there something about you, your company, or your
prospects's past experiences that makes them distrust you?
The real secret to selling is establishing trust in you, your
company, and your product. Personal objections are the most
difficult to handle for several reasons:

- They involve the belief system of the prospect, something difficult to alter in a short time, no matter how irrational those beliefs may be.
- They attack your ego, your self-image, your self-confidence.

Start by putting your ego away. Watch your temper. Don't let your emotions overrule your intellect. This isn't easy to do. After all, if success is personal, how can refusal be abstract? Focus totally on the prospect, not on your own responses. If a prospect is rude or unpleasant, your job is to relax and observe.

When you suspect you are encountering a personal objection, ask, "Is there something about this product or our company that is making you hesitate? Is it something about me personally?" Sometimes prospects will tell you, and sometimes they won't. They may not want to hurt your feelings. When they do tell you, you've collected valuable information for further negotiations.

Make it clear that the most important thing is solving their problem, fixing what is wrong, or helping them reach their goals. If you decide the objection is to you, be ready to try the "T.O." approach, the Turn Over. Somewhere in your presentation, mention the name and prestige of your boss, your field manager, or the owner of the company. Then turn the prospect over to this person. Set up a situation for a callback by someone who may be more acceptable.

The Postponement Objection

Postponement objections come in two forms:

1. Deferred to another decision-maker
2. Thinking it over

Deferred to another decision-maker. A prospect may say, "Well, I'll have to talk it over with my spouse (or my partner or my business associate). That's an objection I hope you never get because it shows you didn't qualify who makes the decisions, either in your pre-call planning or in your approach. Always try to talk to the real buyer. Find out who's "in charge," so that you don't get a postponement objection.

If one does come up, ask to make another presentation with the other party—the buyer, the real decision-maker. No one sells your product or service as well as you do. Don't let someone else make your sales presentation to the actual buyer.

If your prospect absolutely won't let you talk to the decision-maker," then the postponement may be a brush-off, not a real objection. Requalify. If you decide the objection is valid but you still can't get an appointment with the decision-maker, then at least review all the benefits your immediate prospect has agreed to. Make a written list for your prospect to use when presenting your ideas to the committee or the boss. Try to get the prospect to repeat the key points to you before you leave.

Thinking it over. A second postponement objection is "I'll have to think it over." That's very common and often sincere. It is an opportunity for prospects to take time to weigh the pros and cons of your proposal, to decide between options, to convince themselves that going with your product or service is the best thing to do. It's a legitimate objection.

To be sure that prospects *are* considering how your product will benefit them, ask: "Obviously, Mr. Smith, you would not take time to think this over unless you were really interested. Shall we make a list of the points you need to consider?" Use questions to restate the options, benefits, and features. Jot down the ones the prospect wants to think over. Make a second list of points you and the prospect agree on. Summarize these favorable points, compare them to the "under consideration" list, then decide whether to attempt a trial close.

Some other questions to meet postponement objections could be:

- What's going to happen between now and such and such a date that will make a difference?
- What will be more advantageous then?
- Why is June a better time?

Remember that you mustn't seem to be challenging or confronting your prospects. Don't put them on the defensive. You're asking in the spirit of honest inquiry so you can be helpful. Use "Irish questions" to review the benefits you've agreed on so far by turning statements into questions:

- So you feel that our service will deliver better quality than you're currently getting? And you've agreed that the reduced paperwork will be a major benefit for you? And our price is well within your budget? So the only undecided issue is how you will resolve your contractual arrangement with your current supplier? When do you think you'll be able to talk to your legal department about that? Shall I check back with you on Thursday? You think that could be cleared up by March?

Try to pinpoint and solve the problems standing in the way of their making a decision. If the problem is financial, you could say:

- If I could show you how this improvement would pay for itself within a year, would you want to get started next week?
- If we can arrange to delay payments until the end of the quarter (or when you've completed this big job, etc.) would you like to be up and running next week and pay for it as it pays for itself?
- If I could help you solve that one problem, would using our service be a good step for your business right now?

Questions like these can help prospects clarify their own thinking about postponement objections.

Isolate Objections

Professional salespeople rarely encounter any objections because they have already eliminated them with skilled qualifying, patient probing, and a solid presentation. However, when they do, their motto is "Divide and conquer."

Isolate objections. Don't accept vague complaints or broad negative statements as valid objections. Get the prospect to clarify the objection until you both agree on its exact substance. Be sure to praise objecting prospects for their perceptiveness and understanding of the issues.

- Is that the only reason? What other reasons would you have to . . . ." (Not "Is there any other reason?" Assume that there is.)
- Why do you think your managers are opposed to doing it that way?
- Are you seeing something that's not up to your standards?
- Is that the only thing holding you back?
- There's no way you'd reconsider this option...or is there?
- So you've absolutely decided against our product? What factors made up your mind?

Use questions to keep focusing prospects on their real objections. Then use skilled questions to overcome the objection. You can literally question them into a sale.

"We've Already Got One"

George Nicholson, vice president of marketing and sales for Software Solutions in Atlanta, was demonstrating their systems at a trade show. One man watched the demo and then said, "That really looks good, but we can't buy it. We've already spent a great deal of money on a customized system designed by someone in our company."

George asked: "If you had this program, exactly how would you use it?" George's next question: "Is it a top management responsibility to cut losses when things are wrong and to change to new systems, new techniques, and even new employees if circumstances demand it?"

"Yes."

"If you had an employee who wasn't doing the job, would you let him go or keep paying his salary?"

"Let him go."

"Isn't it time that you retired the old customized system that is less efficient, and hired this new system that will really do the job?" George stayed very quiet and waited for an answer. He could see the wheels turning and eventually the man replied, "Come to my office next Tuesday and show this product to our other executives. I think we want to do it." They bought it. Then twenty-five more systems were purchased during the next year through their referrals. In all, twenty-six separate deals were consummated, a $1,300,000 gross in one year through a single contact.

"I Got Burned Before!"

What can you say to a prospect who has sworn off your entire industry because of a bad experience? Maybe you have the best product or service in the world, but the prospect doesn't want to hear about it. In fact you may get an earful yourself as the prospect dumps all the built-up anger and resentment from this past disaster. It's easy to slink away and try another prospect.

Before you do, you might want to try a question similar to one my son, Bill Bethel Jr., uses in his telephone selling strategy, currently for Crystal Falls Marketing. He listens sympathetically to the angry denunciation, commiserates, then asks, "But do you want to let this one awful experience keep you from ever having these benefits? *If you had a bad steak in a restaurant, would you stop eating steak?*" Seventy percent of the time this question gets the prospect to stop objecting and listen to the rest of the story.

He then goes on to show how his product has none of the drawbacks of the bad one. By listening to the prospect's frustration and hostility, he has established a "common ground" of shared experience. Then he is able to use the prospect's negative energy in a positive way by pointing out the features and benefits of his product.

Revise Your Presentation?

The professional salesperson's goal is to answer all objections before they are raised. How do you do that? You design your presentation to cover every possible objection you can imagine. When you do your pre-call planning, predict objections. If you are new to your company or your product, ask a senior salesperson for help. Ask, "What kind of objections do you run into most?"

Then you should:

- Design questions that will lead prospects to overcoming their own objections.
- Learn how to ask.
- Learn when to ask.

You'll still get an objection once in a while. When the same objection comes up more than once, you should consider modifying your presentation to cover that point. Build in the questions that meet the objection before it arises.

"Questions are a great confidence builder. Salespeople who are confident ask a lot of questions. You are at your most competitive and effective when you work from knowledge. Can you imagine going to a doctor who doesn't ask you any questions?"

Ron Von Trapp
Director of North
American Sales
Plus Development
Corporation

8

Closing Questions

"What is making you hesitate?"
Revealed the objection that was holding up a $30
million sale. (See page 141.)

---

*"You say some of your people have been
with you for ten years. Then why don't you
owe them the right to choose?"*
Resulted in a $191,000 sale of customized computer
hardware. (See page 149.)

"One egg or two in your milkshake?"
Classic Elmer Wheeler alternate-closing line that
upped profits for thousands of soda fountains.
(See page 150.)

A closing question is any question that confirms that the prospect is willing to buy. This question is rarely: "Will you buy?"

The market place is always changing. Some of the standard closing techniques of the past are now considered questionable, ineffective, or even illegal. Closing today should depend on satisfying and convincing your customers, not confounding and conquering them. Fortunately there are still a half dozen classic, solid, tried-and-true ways to close a sale that really work.

The words you use to close are important, but your close is a lot more than the few seconds you take to ask for the sale. It is the entire sales process, from pre-contact planning to the closed-end question that translates as "Would you like to buy?" Your closing question is just the peak of a triangle, built on the broad base of your service-oriented sales presentation, features and benefits, and asking questions. All through the sales contact you are preparing for the final act of closing.

```
closing
questions
features & benefits
service
```

Closing a sale has been compared to buttoning the last button of an overcoat. As the prospect accepts each benefit, one more button is being buttoned. As you confirm your prospects' needs, wants, desires, fears, and prejudices, you lead them to discover for themselves how your features and benefits will make their lives better. Then it's easy to get to the last button. When you do, you close the sale.

Early Temperature Testers

You've heard of trial closings. There are also pre-trial closings, questions that test prospect interest before you go on to a trial close:

- How does that sound to you?
- What haven't I covered to your satisfaction? (Not "Have I covered everything to your satisfaction?")
- Is your home office going to have any problem with this?
- Can you think of any other solution that would work better for you?

When you get favorable answers to questions like these, you are ready to go on to a real closing question. When there are no more objections, the sale should follow automatically.

But what if it isn't clear that the prospect *has* any objections and the sale is still stalled? Bob Denman, an account representative for a major computer services company, ran into that problem with a leading personal property and casualty company. Bob felt that he had met and overcome all objections, yet the decision-maker didn't make a decision. Finally Bob confronted him: "What makes you hesitate about doing business with us right now?"

> *He replied that there was another company in the running and he wasn't sure we could deliver and service their account as well as this competitor. "Is there any other reason?" I asked. "No." That let me concentrate our selling efforts on this objection. We convinced him and got their business. Our share is approximately $30 million in gross revenues, worldwide.*

Use your pre-closing questions to look for hidden objections, objections that even your prospect may not be aware of.

Sixteen Classic Closings

You can lead a horse to water, but it may not do much good unless you have made it mighty thirsty on the way. Here are sixteen classic closings:

1. Trial close
2. Assumptive close
3. Alternate-choice close
4. Action close
5. Inducement close
6. Summary close
7. Benjamin Franklin close
8. Minor-point close
9. Reduce to one objection close.
10. Fear-of-loss close
11. Unanswered objection close

12. Upgrade closing
13. Callback closing
14. End-of-the-trail close
15. Subordinate close
16. One-more-thing close

Closing is when you do something that your prospect responds to by doing something final. It's a cause-and-effect relationship. You say, "R-O-L-A-I-D-S" and someone completes the phrase with " . . . spells relief." Or you pluck the petals from a daisy, saying: "She loves me, she loves me not . . . ." And then you hold out the flower to your beloved with just one petal remaining. If she picks it, she loves you. That's a close.

Trial Close

A trial close is a real close that maybe isn't. It's like a thermometer, checking the prospect's temperature. If the prospect is hot and responds positively, you've closed the sale. If the prospect is only lukewarm, you haven't lost any ground.

- John, in your opinion, is this five-point security system the best one for your Boston plant?
- How are your people going to feel about the changes these new terminals will produce? (Not "would produce.")
- What's your gut reaction to replacing this unit instead of trying to keep it repaired?

A trial close asks questions about opinions and feelings, not about decisions. You know when you have reached closing if you take your prospects' buying temperature along the way. Ask questions to find how you are progressing in your presentation. A "no" on a trial close means: "Give me more information. Explain that better. Clarify."

You can do this with the *Feel-Felt-Found* strategy. Say, "I know how you *feel*" or "I can see why you're thinking that way. Lots of my clients *felt* the same way, and they *found* that . . . . " That's Feel-Felt-Found. Then restate your benefits. Show people that you know how they feel, understand their reservations, and have complete respect for their current convictions. Help your prospects to identify with others who once felt the same way. Then explain how others changed their minds and demonstrate the results they have achieved by taking your advice.

Assumptive Close

Use the assumptive close only after a trial close indicates that the prospect is receptive. If you use it too early, you risk irritating the prospect and aborting the entire presentation.

A common key word in the assumptive close is "When." You ask when the prospect wants or will use your product: "From what you've said, you need delivery tomorrow. May I use your phone to see if we can meet your schedule." When prospects say yes, they are in effect agreeing to the purchase. Some typical assumptive closes would be:

- So June 1st would be a good starting date?
- Will three be enough for the time being?
- What delivery date is good for you?
- How long would you like the warranty to run?
- Would you like our people to install that for you?
- Do you want us to load it in your car?

But what if you risk an assumptive close and the prospect jumps back, saying "Hold everything! I never said I was going to buy!" ? Great. Treat this exchange as a trial close. Ask questions to find out what is stopping the sale, then return to handling objections.

A nice addition to the assumptive close is the *third-party close*, AKA the *testimonial close*. You show your prospect how someone else benefited from and recommends your product, and you assume they will want to do the same.

Another variation is the *order blank close*. It's the oldest one in the world and the nicest. It combines the Assumptive and Action closes: You simply take out an order form and start writing. Prospects who aren't ready to buy will say so, but you'll be surprised how few people will stop you—that is, if you've given excellent service and a presentation tailored to their needs and concerns.

With the assumptive close you assume that your prospect has agreed with all the points during the presentation. There can be a magic and power in this attitude that is contagious. If you are assumptive as you go through the presentation you'll find many prospects more ready to buy.

Of course the professional salesperson takes for granted that a prospect is going to buy, now or in the future, but correct use of the assumptive close can be tricky and requires extra sensitivity.

Alternate-Choice Close

The alternate-choice is an advance on the trial close. Use it when you are fairly certain of receptivity. You ask:

- Would you like to schedule your people for our full-support training program *before* or *after* installation of the new equipment?
- Would you like six now and we'll hold the other six for delivery until you need them? Or would you rather have us send all twelve together?
- Would you like to order another gross and get the quantity discount?
- Will this be check or charge?
- Shall we send it by UPS or Express Mail?
- Do you want to handle the paperwork or shall I?
- Do you want to pick that up or shall we deliver it?
- Would you prefer a service contract or an extended warranty?
- Do you need to get a purchase order or is your signature sufficient?

An alternate-choice close offers your prospects some suitable options. If appropriate for your product or service, prepare a list of alternate-choice closes to use at the end of your presentation.

Action Close

This close asks the prospect to respond physically to what you are saying. For example, you might fill out an order form and say, "Here's what we've found you need, Mr. Jordan. If you'll verify it, we can arrange delivery for Tuesday." Or ". . . so that's how much you'll save. Shall we go ahead on that basis?"

- Would you check this list and see if it covers all your immediate needs?
- Shall we walk this over to purchasing for a signature so we can set up immediate delivery?
- Would your foreman like a chance to check this out today?
- How about taking the model down to your shop right now and I'll have the rest delivered next week?
- Would you like to receive our 5% discount by ordering one more?
- Do you want to save on shipping by ordering an extra one now?

When prospects agree that everything is exactly as they want it, you say, "And your signature goes there . . . ." (Notice that you may never have said, "Will you buy?")

Inducement Close

Create an inducement to buy now. Popular inducement closes are offering special airfares or school tuition reductions if payment is made well in advance. Inducements can be in the form of a bonus for immediate action. Seminar organizer John Hammond offers free bonus lectures for participants who sign up for the main attractions before a certain date.

- Would you like to save 15 percent by booking before July 1st?
- Do you want to stock up? The price goes up on Sunday.

One of my early clients told me why she chose me over my competitors although we all offered similar prices and services: "You give the best Christmas party."

Summary Close

Often combined with an assumptive or action close: "Now let me summarize what you will be getting." Relist the points of agreement and confirm them with the prospect as you go. When enough points have been agreed to, you either assume the sale has been completed or you take action by handing the prospect a pen.

Benjamin Franklin Close

I love the Ben Franklin close. It is a valuable tool that has made me a great deal of money over the years. Ben was noted for his careful weighing of all the factors involved before he made a decision. For the Ben Franklin close, take a sheet of paper and draw a vertical line down the center. Label one side "For" and the other side "Against." Get your prospect to help you list all the "For" benefits, all the reasons your prospect should buy. Then ask your prospect to fill in all the points against buying under "Against."

Now here is the secret of the Ben Franklin close. You, the knowledgeable salesperson, are well prepared to remind your prospect of the many benefits. The "For" list usually has eight, ten, or twelve points because you suggest them. The prospect's "Against" column has only three or four if you've been doing good job. The preponderance of the evidence is on your side of the page when you use a Ben Franklin close.

Your next statement is a question: "If we could resolve these three objections to your satisfaction, would you purchase now?" Then answer those objections.

Minor-Point Close

What if prospects seem to be rejecting every major point in your presentation? You can still work your way to a sale by using the minor-point close. Start by getting agreement on any small point for which it's easy to get agreement. When they've said "yes" to many minor points, it's easier to get them to go along with the major decision, the final purchase. It diffuses objections to larger issues if you get them to agree to little things first.

Reduce-to-One-Objection Close

Here you try to eliminate all objections except one. You put that one aside for the moment because you know you have the solution to that objection.

- Except for money, can you think of any reason not to go ahead right now?
- Besides the turn-around time, what else would keep you from using our service?
- If it weren't for the high maintenance on this model, would it be perfect for your application?

Your ace-in-the-hole is that you can offer favorable financing terms, faster turn-around, or a new low maintenance model. Let's say your company has the best financing plan in the industry: no down payment, no payments for sixty days, and a very low monthly payment compared to the competition. All the way through your presentation, you'll say: "Except for the cost, is there any reason you'd choose our competitor's model over ours? Setting cost aside, are there any features you need that this doesn't have? If it weren't for money, can you think of anything that would stop you from going ahead?" Then you meet and overcome every other objection.

When Ron Von Trapp was with NBI, they were trying to get a $2 million order from a major Hollywood studio. As part of information gathering, he asked if he could work a few days for the studio so he could better understand how they functioned.

> *On the lot where they kept all the props I found twenty-five huge cameras, covered with dust. "What are these doing here?" I asked. "Well, we just keep them in reserve in case they're*

needed. Mostly they just sit." I asked what they cost. "About $200,000 each."

Two months later during a formal presentation, I found that information very useful. The president said he'd like to do a trial implementation —have us put in several hundred thousand dollars worth equipment and see how it worked before they decided to place the full order. We were convinced this was the wrong approach.

So I said, "Over in your lot I found twenty-five big cameras in storage. Do you know what they cost?"

He said, "No."

"They cost $200,000 each," I told him. "You've got about $5 million worth of cameras sitting there. I have an idea for you to consider. Would it be a better use of your money to sell ten of those cameras to pay $2 million for a system that's going to deliver all these benefits to your organization?"

"This stuff better work!" he said and he signed the contract.

Reduce and reduce until you hold the winning card. Eventually your prospect has only one objection left, the one you feel confident you can overcome.

Fear-of-Loss Close

People are more motivated by fear of loss than by hope for gain. Look around you. There are thousands of examples of that everywhere. Be sure during your presentation that your prospects understand what they risk losing if they don't act.

You can sometimes use the fear-of-loss close in combination with the impending event close. You point out something about to happen that could result in a loss for the prospect.

- Do you like this color? It's been discontinued and we've only got these left.
- Did last year's storms catch you unprepared? What kind of damage did you have? Are you ready for this year?
- How soon do you need your people to get this training? We have fourteen openings in the June 2nd workshop, but after that there won't be another seminar until September.

You inform or remind prospects of coming events that may cause them a loss if they don't act.

Unanswered-Objection Close

If something is keeping your prospect from saying "yes," take a direct approach: "What is standing in the way of our doing business now? Is there anything that I can do that would get you to say 'yes'?"

Ron Von Trapp was trying to sell a computer system to a major university in southern California. Ron is director of North American Sales for Plus Development Corporation. The university's decision-maker for this sale was the dean of the medical school:

> *Everyone there agreed that my system was a much better solution—everyone except the dean who preferred another system. It was very frustrating.*
>
> *One of the selling points of the simpler system he favored was that it is easier for new employees to learn in high-turnover situations. However my questioning had shown that this university had very low turnover, both administrative and clerical.*
>
> *Finally I met with the dean and said, "I want to ask you two questions. If you can give me good answers, I'll leave. First, what's your turnover like?" He admitted that they had very low*

*turnover and many employees had been there
ten years.*

*"Then," I said, "as one professional to an-
other, why is it that you don't owe these people
their own decision? You tell me they are dedi-
cated, loyal, hard working, and they want this
system. Please explain to me why you don't feel
obligated to honor their decision?" Now, if
he'd given me some silly answer, I'd have continued. But he didn't. He bought my system.*

"I always close with questions," says Ron, "and I have a
very high close ratio." You can see why.

Confrontation is a last resort close. Use it only when
you're dealing with a terminally indecisive prospect. You'll
get an answer one way or the other, so you can get down to
business or get on to the next prospect.

Upgrade or Add-On Close

Elmer Wheeler (the man who advised selling the "sizzle" not
the steak) upped sales of milk shakes by asking "would you
like one egg or two with your shake?"

- Would you like to buy a case and get the twelfth can free?
- Can I show you a shirt and tie to go with your new suit?
- If you could choose a second one free, which would it be?

Supermarkets know the value of add-on sales. They keep
racks of candy, magazines, batteries, and other impulse items
next to the cash register where they can easily be added to
your cart while you wait.

Callback Close

Use callback closes when you call on the same prospect or
customer repeatedly. A callback close is actually a complete
presentation. Even though you've already done full presentations for the prospect or this is a regular customer, don't
assume they remember everything you said before or that

their situation is the same. Start at the beginning. Rebuild rapport. Go through all the steps of the sales process, compressing them based on your prospect's responses. Review all the major points that you have covered before. Ask if anything has changed. Be sure the prospect knows that you are interested in serving their needs, solving their problems, fixing what is wrong, then use your other closes to get the sale.

End-of-the-Trail Close

If a prospect keeps stalling you, telling you to call back and call back and call back, sooner or later you'll want to use the end-of-the-trail hard close: "Have you decided now? Do you want to buy?" It's time to win it or lose it. Old-timers in the life insurance business know the motto: "China eggs never hatch no matter how long you sit on them."

Subordinate Close

This is similar to the minor point close and could be interchanged. For example, don't ask, "Do you want to buy?" Ask, "What more can I do to make sure you are happy with this purchase?"

One-More-Thing Close

After the prospect has said "no" and you are about to part, say: "Oh, one more thing . . . ." Then ask a question based on the benefits they have already accepted.

One-more-thing closes are also useful in turnover situations. (Turnovers are very popular in multiple salesperson situations like automobile showrooms.) Keith Sheffield, who worked for me as a salesperson in new housing subdivisions, was a genius at building rapport, answering questions and demonstrating. However, I'll never know if Keith could close. He brought every prospect into my office and left me to ask for the order. That is a turnover, a T.O., a one-more-thing close. When prospects say "no," turn them over to someone else. Let the new salesperson try.

The Four Major Closing Mistakes

Even experienced salespeople sometimes make one of the four most common closing mistakes.

Closing Too Early

A successful closing depends not only on what you ask but when and how you ask it. Take the classic three-word close: "Stick 'em up!" Delivered in a dark, deserted alley, it is nearly 100 percent successful. But delivered in the crowded lobby of a hotel that is hosting a police convention, its chance of success is diminished. If you haven't led your prospects into that imaginary alley, confirmed their eagerness to be there, and made sure no one else is going to make them a better offer, your closing question may be unproductive.

Closing Too Late

Ask professional salespeople, "What is the most important thing about closing?" and most will say, "Don't wait too long." You can literally talk yourself out of a sale by stretching out the presentation and putting off the decision.

Old-time political bosses instructed their cronies to "vote early and often." My first sales manager paraphrased that motto more positively when he told me to "close early and often." Professional salespeople work hard to develop the technique and timing needed for a successful close.

Some salespeople don't close early enough and often enough because don't want to appear too aggressive. However, if you are a truly service-oriented salesperson, caring, empathetic, and concerned for your prospect, then you probably won't seem aggressive when you close. It's not so much what you do as how you do it, not so much what you ask as how you ask it. What you believe to be your good manners may actually be a fear of rejection. Remember that prospects can never reject *you*. They can only refuse your offer.

Talking Past Closing Time

All through each sales contact you will be asking trial-closing questions. When you finally get to the real closing question, ask it and then stop. Be absolutely silent. The one who talks first always loses.

This is where inexperienced salespeople "buy back" their product or service. They are afraid of the silence that follows a closing question, so they jump in and start talking again. Many sales are lost by talking past the magic moment.

Not Closing at All

Some salespeople confuse building rapport with socializing. They don't know why they are with the prospect. I knew one man who could enchant his prospects but he was so afraid of losing a sale that he never got around to asking for it. Remember the rule: *Refusal is not rejection.*

One study indicated that 63% of sales presentations end without the salesperson ever asking for the sale. I have seen salespeople give a flawless presentation and then never ask a closing question. Don't waste all your work, all your preparation, all your time by being afraid to ask the closing question.

The Courage NOT to Make the Sale

The ultimate closing may be no closing at all. What if your questions reveal that your prospect doesn't need what you are selling. That is an ethical problem that every salesperson faces sooner or later. I talked to Timothy Murphy, sales manager for a major industrial textile fabricator, right after he had one such experience:

*If you're really listening to what your prospects
are saying about their problem, the right solution may be to do nothing. Just yesterday I
passed on a bid where it was better for the
customer to have new signage put on the existing canopy than to recover it. If I had listened
only to what he thought he wanted—if I hadn't
asked "What do you expect to accomplish?
What is your budget? What are you trying to
do?"—he'd have been $3,500 poorer and I
would not have done him a service or increased
his income. Then the next time he needed a
canopy, I wouldn't get a phone call.*

*You've got to do what you're doing with
honesty, dignity, and pride. If you can't, go find
something else to do. Part of solving a
prospect's problem may mean you don't sell
them something.*

Closing the Closing

Your prospect has agreed to buy. You are confident that your
product or service is the right one at the right price for the
prospect's needs. There are still three things you must do to
truly close the sale.

1. Outline each other's tasks and responsibilities.
2. Work out an implementation schedule.
3. Reconfirm all the details of the sale: quantities, sizes,
   price, delivery, discounts, extra charges, etc. Don't *assume* anything. Clarify now to avoid disaster later.

John Patterson, often called the dean of sales trainers, told
his National Cash Register salesmen to try for a close seven

times before they turned in a report that a prospect couldn't be sold.

Your ability to become a proficient closer will come with experience. Get started. Learn to close early and often. Make mistakes. Win some, lose some. Soon you'll develop that sense of timing that produces a high closing ratio.

"Without questions, the sales process can fall apart before it begins. When I hire a salespeople, I always ask them what they feel are the characteristics of a good salesperson. The one answer I look for more than any other is the ability to be a good listener. By inference that suggests they are asking questions."

Rich Goldman
Senior Vice President
and General Sales
Manager
Television Program
Enterprises,
a division of Cox
Enterprises

9

Follow-Up Questions

*"How did last Thursday's spots pull in
Brooklyn?"*
Turned a small trial order for radio time into a major
client. (See page 157.)

---

*"What's the best investment you've ever
made?"*
Sold four homes to same client. (See page 163.)

"Is there any way I could look around a bit?"
Recovered a lost $100,000 sale. (See page 164.)

Making a sale is the total of all the steps you go through.
It starts the moment you first consider contacting the prospect
and ends with your post-sale follow-up that confirms they are
completely satisfied with their purchase.

You've got to sell *after* you make the sale. When Allison
Wilson was an account executive with WNEW in New York
City, she took a call from a trucking company in Yonkers.

> *In fact, I made the initial sale on my second
> week at the station. I was all alone in the office
> late on the Friday before the Fourth of July
> weekend when a call came in. The client
> placed a small trial order to run during the New
> York Giants Broadcast. We were successful
> with this client because we really followed up.
> We monitored their progress and success in the*

*different day parts. I continued asking questions
to find out which spots were pulling and which
were not. Then we moved their spots to increase the response. I kept asking questions to
make sure we were servicing them, that they
were pleased with everything. I didn't want
them to be just a New York Giants sponsor. I
wanted them fifty-two weeks a year.*

They became one of her top three sales: "It was the right questions that did it."

Six Ways to Keep Customers

You keep customers when you show that you really care about them and their needs.

Know them well.

There is no substitute for using both business and personal information to convince your customers that you are truly interested in their feelings and their needs. Keep a record—a computerized list or a card file—with a history of your sales contacts, what they've bought, what they are likely to buy in the future. Most of all, record personal data about their family, hobbies, likes and dislikes, birthdays, anniversaries and any special occasions.

About a dozen years ago I had a business contact with a salesman named Addison Dwyer. I have not seen Addison for twelve years, but every year I receive a phone call from him on my birthday. I'm always amazed that he remembers and takes the time to call me. Does it make me feel important? It sure does. Does it help him? It sure does. Whenever I have an opportunity to sing his praises, refer prospects to him, or purchase his product, he is the salesperson I remember be-cause he remembers me.

Remember that the palest ink is stronger than the strong-est memory. Learn all you can about your customer and develop a written system to remind you of the things that are important to them.

Contact them often.

Use personal contact, post cards or telephone calls—whatever is appropriate. Maintain a record of these contacts and note when you should make another follow-up. Constantly say "Thank you"—in person, in writing, on the phone. Is there something that you can congratulate them for? Promotions, birthdays, graduations? Can you just call to say, "hello, I was thinking of you" ?

Joe Gerard, one of the most famous and successful automobile salespeople of all time, said that he sent 14,000 postcards per *week* to remind people of him and his product. What are you doing to be remembered?

Be available to your customers. Some people think that salespeople work only four days a week, that they always play golf on Friday. The tireless Ron Von Trapp makes a point of dropping in on two or three of his customers every Friday afternoon: "That floors them. I walk in unannounced and say, 'Hi, I just wanted to see how everything is going.' I have never lost a customer to a competitor once I have them. There is not one single customer in twenty-three years that I cannot go back to and get a good reference."

Handle complaints promptly.

Problems are a wonderful opportunity to cement customer relations. Take no complaint lightly, no matter how trivial, and follow through immediately.

Raymond Gatheral is a salesperson for Advanced Paper Systems in San Jose, California. One of Raymond's clients complained that a small shipping charge was several times higher than the rate they were used to paying. Raymond didn't argue. He said, "We will reverse the charge immediately." The next month the client was again charged. Raymond contacted the client immediately and said that not only would the charge be reversed, but in the future they would not be charged for shipping on that type of order. He instructed the bookkeeper to post on this client's record: "All shipping without charge." He told his company that if that wasn't acceptable, they should deduct this client's shipping charges from his commission account. Now, *that* is handling complaints and settling problems promptly.

Keep your promises.

Prove you are dependable by making a promise and then keeping it. People who feel good about themselves do better in their selling careers. Isn't self-esteem based on your feelings about *you?* When you keep your promise, you influence the confidence and trust of your client while you reinforce your own belief in yourself.

Serve!

Make yourself indispensable. Customers never leave a supplier if they can't afford to. Your job as a professional salesperson is to make sure there is an advantage for doing business with you. Do you sometimes stretch yourself to give your customers the attention they deserve? Do you make sure their orders are filled and delivered properly? Do you stay in touch, by phone or in person, to see how things are going? Do you stay aware of their changing needs so you can adjust the way you serve them? Do you give follow-up service to maintain the relationship and insure satisfaction?

Beg.

Demonstrate their value and importance to you by asking them to do you a favor: "Maybe you can help me?" As I said in Chapter 1, everyone wants to help. Ask for something, maybe even a sale: "What can I do to get you to purchase your next system from me?"

Confirm Your Relationship

Start by being sure that everything about the customer's initial reaction is positive:

- How are you doing with the new widgit?
- Was your delivery on time?
- Is it performing the way you expected?
- How would you rate our service? Is everything going okay?
- Are your people having any problems?

Continue by confirming and reinforcing benefits:

- What kind of speed (or quantityor time saving) are you getting now? Do you have any hard figures? Is that what you hoped for?
- How are your people responding to the new system? Is this reaction you expected? What other feedback have you had?

Show you are thinking about their needs:

- Is your current arrangement still giving you trouble?
- I've just gotten something that I think might solve your problem. Shall I come by tomorrow so you can take a look at it? (Or, would you like me to send the specs over?)
- Are you running low on any supplies?
- Is this a good time to rethink your system? You talked about it several months ago and I've got some suggestions for you if you're ready . . . ?

Be a problem-solver and a trouble-shooter. Be sure that you are notified if any problem arises:

- I hear you called our customer service department with a problem . . . ? (Wait to hear if a problem really existed and if it has been resolved. If not, *solve* it!)
- What kind of service did you get from our repair department (or billing department or installers or trainers)? Is there any way you think this could be improved? Should I talk directly to the person who had the problem to see if I can help?
- What additional supports do you need from us?

Collect data that will make you and your company better able to serve:

- I know we're just one of your suppliers. (Or, I know you've looked at other companies with similar services.) How do you think we compare?
- How is your new system interfacing with your old equipment? Do you see any problems down the road?
- Who else is going to be using this? What's the best way for me to interact with them?

Finally, use your follow-up as a springboard to future sales:

- Have you found new needs as you've used it?
- Has increased production created new needs in your department? How can we help you to meet these new requirements?
- Have you found new ways to use our product? What new kinds of applications do you think we should consider?
- Who else do you think could use this?

A Dynamite Follow-Up Letter

Exercise machines are hot right now and Nordic Track makes one of the most popular. They sell mostly by direct marketing or through their own retail dealerships, and count on referrals. I purchased a Nordic Track and received a great follow-up letter:

> *How about you? Are you feeling healthier and stronger lately? More relaxed and more energetic? Congratulations. You've discovered how it pays to get fit and stay fit through total body exercise on your Nordic Track. Now I'd like you to consider sharing your special knowledge with a friend or relative . . . .*
>
> *We thank you for your continued support and your friends will thank you for helping with*

> their fitness goals of looking and feeling their
> best and being the very best they can be.

(In addition, Nordic owners are offered a less altruistic inducement. This letter offers a $100 savings bond for every referral who buys a Nordic Track exercise machine.)

What Is a Customer Worth?

What does it cost you *not* to keep a customer? Usually it is more cost-effective to retain a customer than get a new one. Richard P. Cooley, CEO of Seafirst Corporation, estimates that "the average cost of acquiring a (bank) customer—including marketing, advertising, opening a credit account—ranges from $500 to $1000." Acquiring a new customer costs money, but usually the longer they stay with you, the more they spend with you. Operating costs drop because both customer and company learn what to expect from each other. "Companies can boost profits by almost 100 percent by retaining just 5 percent more of their customers," says Cooley.

The dollar value of retaining a customer for even small-ticket items may surprise you. For example, Phil Bressler, co-owner of five Domino's Pizza stores in Montgomery Country, Maryland, has calculated that a regular customer is worth more then $5,000 over the life of a ten-year franchise contract. He emphasizes that figure to every Domino's employee, from manager to order taker.

Obviously if follow-ups retain customers, they are cost-effective, but what constitutes a follow-up? The realtor who sold us a house some years ago followed up by us sending flowers and inviting us out to dinner. Then she never contacted us again. She figured we had bought our house and would have no more need of her, so she'd better spend her time cultivating new prospects.

A few months later another realtor we had worked with, called us. He asked how we were doing and if we were happy with our choice. We chatted briefly about the neighborhood and how we were settling in. Over the years he stayed in touch with us. When our relatives and employees were ready to buy homes, we referred them to him, not the realtor who had handled our own sale. When we were ready to make an investment, we turned to him because he had *asked* us to think about how to make our money grow: "What's the best investment you've ever made?" We agreed that residential property in California was one of the best investments it was possible to make at the time. Over the years he sold at least five properties as a direct result of those follow-up contacts with us.

Between hamburgers and houses there is a vast middle ground for repeat sales and regular customers. A 1990 article in the *Harvard Business Review* by Frederick F. Reichheld and W. Earl Sasser Jr. said that "it is common for a business to lose 15 percent to 20 percent of its customers each year." Some lose considerably more than that. If you cut your defection rate in half, what would that mean in sales each year?

The $100,000 Comeback Question

Follow-up is usually defined as what you do *after* the sale, but it can also be anything you do that recovers an all-but-lost sale. Dr. James Penton discovered this when a lifetime passion became the catalyst for a dramatic recovery. His job is to provide technical support for one of the top scientific instrument manufacturers in the U.S. In this capacity he often accompanies salespeople on calls.

> *I've been a space buff since I was a small child, so when we made a sales call at Rockwell's space shuttle station in Palmdale, California, I felt like a kid in a candy store. When the prospect led us through the assembly building and I got to walk under an actual shuttle, all I could think was "Wow!"*
>
> *In the purchaser's office, our salesperson began his memorized presentation. Now this man was the kind who has read every book on*

selling ever published and studied every selling technique. He got so caught up in his pre-programmed presentation that he forgot the prospect was there. He had become a scripted robot. Neither the prospect nor I could have broken in with an axe. As the prospect started to squirm and glance at his watch, I could see a $100,000 sale slowly but surely slipping away.

Finally the prospect announced that he would miss his carpool if we continued, and he showed us the door. As we were on our way out, I risked asking a question: "Gee, I've been following space flights since I was a boy. I know you have to go, but is there any way I could look around a bit?"

Immediately the prospect decided that he had enough time to take us on a tour. I continued asking excited questions about everything we saw for almost an hour. As we were leaving, the prospect said, "If you're this interested, you must be very knowledgeable." We got the order.

Skillful follow-up questioning may help you make a comeback when someone—even you—has effectively lost the sale.

Whether you are trying to recover a client's interest during the sales process or trying to keep your customer after the order has been filled, become a follow-up expert. Build a sound relationship so your clients turn to you first as their resource.

Can you send tearsheets or photocopies of articles that suggest ways to use your product? Can you write such an article? Can you call your clients to tell them how other customers are using the product? Can you visit or send a letter just to stay in touch?

Ask yourself: After the check is cashed and the product delivered, how important is the customer now? Some salespeople sit back, take a deep breath, and congratulate themselves. However, the professional salesperson knows that the job *really* begins after closing.

"I use a lot of questions after I've made the sale and delivered the product.

- *Was it a good decision?*
- *Does it do what we thought it would?*
- *Are you happy?*
- *Where do we go from here?*

If you've got this kind of contact and you've made a mistake, you can fix it quickly."

Ron Von Trapp
Director of North
American Sales
Plus Development
Corporation

10

What Is a Professional?

"Why did you ask that question?"
Procured a contract with a 132-store chain.
(See page 171.)

_____

"What are you doing at 5:00 A.M.?"
Earned a $100,000 sale from a hard-to-pin-down
prospect. (See page 172.)

_____

"What should I do now?"
Persuaded an "I won't buy anything!" fund manager
to invest $500,000. (See page 173.)

Since medieval times there have been only four professions: law, medicine, religion, and higher academia. Their practitioners were called "professionals" because they had to profess or swear an oath. In more recent times professional came to mean "not an amateur." If you were paid, you were a professional. If you did it for free, you were an amateur. Today professionalism has a whole new meaning. It is not the job you do, it's how you do the job.

Have you ever said to someone, "Boy, you're a real pro!" or "You do that like a pro" ? Do you want to hear your clients say that to you? Being a professional in sales means that you combine vision, knowledge, and drive with sensitivity and nuts- and-bolts know-how. It means doing the right thing at the right time for the right reason. To know what to do, when to do it, and why to do it, professional salespeople ask questions. They ask themselves, they ask their prospects, they ask their clients, and they ask other salespeople.

James Thurber said, "It is better to know some of the questions than all of the answers." I learned this when, as a fledgling salesperson, I approached my sales manager with my first questions:

BB: Where is the best place to get a list of people who might buy from me?

SM: I don't know. Lists have never worked for me.

BB: Well, should I ask my friends to buy?

SM: I'm not sure. I've always felt you should keep your business and social life separate.

BB: If I can get an appointment, should I qualify to be sure they have the money?

SM: That's risky. I don't know if I'd qualify too strongly.

BB: By the way, I hope you don't mind my asking all these questions?

SM: Not at all. How else are you going to learn?

That sounds like a comedy routine, but it's very close to the truth. Not everyone knows all the answers, but just asking can get the juices flowing.

Which Questions Work?

Questions work, but knowing which question and when to ask it is the key to your sales success. Start keeping a record of the ones that work for *you*. How did your prospect respond? What important information did you get from the responses? How did they help get the sale? Use a computer file, a card file, or notebook to keep track. You should also jot down questions that *didn't* work. Why didn't they? What would you do differently next time?

Ten Question-Asking Don'ts

Sometimes it's not what you ask but *how*. No matter what your questions, there are some ways to ask that you should learn to avoid.

1. *Don't* give anyone the third degree.
2. *Don't* ask questions too quickly. Pause for answers.
3. *Don't* ignore the answer to a question and continue down a memorized mental list. Always make your next question responsive to the prospect's answer to your last question.
4. *Don't* ask deceptive questions.
5. *Don't* ask prying questions.
6. *Don't* ask trivial questions.
7. *Don't* ask sarcastic questions.
8. *Don't* ask embarrassing questions.
9. *Don't* ask uninteresting questions.
10. *Don't* ask antagonistic questions.

Like anything powerful, questions must be used wisely, carefully, and skillfully. Think of them as a key, not a club.

Which Type of Sales for You?

All selling can be divided into three types—I hesitate to say "levels" because that implies that one is somehow better than another. Each type is vital to the selling process that maintains our economy, and all three attract top professionals. Each area of selling uses different kinds of questions and different questioning and listening techniques, but all rely on basic questioning skills.

The majority of salespeople work in the first two categories of selling.

The Product Sale

You want to sell this single product to this person right now. Emphasis is on the salesperson's needs and wants, not those of the customer. The car insurance salesman wants to find someone who owns a car and needs insurance. The hot dog vendor is eager to find a hungry person with the price of a hot dog and is not concerned about the prospects' overall nutritional, emotional, or social needs. Emphasis is on good prospecting, attention-getting, and motivational questions about immediate needs.

The Need-based Consultive Sale

This is what Dr. Tony Alessandra calls "non-manipulative" selling. This is the inverted pyramid. You gather information through probing questions, then try to fit your product to a person's real needs, wants, and desires. The close follows almost automatically. Your questions build a successful sales relationship. The need-based sale implies that you are offering a range of options.

You become a consultant to your customers. You learn a great deal about their business and operations through probing questions, then advise them on how they can best use your product. You give them information that solves their problems or helps them achieve their objectives.

The Resource Sale

When you become a resource to your clients, you are almost out of "selling" as we normally think of it. Manufacturer's rep Paula Ebejer, the territory manager with Bradshaw North food brokers (page 115), often acts as a resource. Frank Snowden is a manufacturer's rep selling Fisher Mountain bikes, clothing, and Avocet bike accessories (page 22). He walks into a retail store and looks around on the shelf, sees how many they have of each thing, automatically restocks, tells them what the competition is doing, what other stores are doing for promotion, and takes away the rejects. He becomes a full partner with the business, as if he were a co-owner.

Can You Answer Unvoiced Questions?

Every time you answer a prospect's question, be on the lookout for an unvoiced question-behind-the-question. The prospect may be fishing for very different information. Ed Ayd, senior account manager for Dataserv, told me how he handled a classic example. Dataserv provides support for custom-tailored computer systems and backups. During a presentation, one prospect asked Ed: "What would you do if your representative was driving to one of my stores in upstate New York that had a critical problem and his car went off the road?" Ed told her that if the car couldn't be back on the road within fifteen or twenty minutes, they would immediately send a backup person.

> Then I asked her, "Why did you ask that question?" That's a question I ask a lot. The moment of truth. She said, "Because your competition has told me that you don't have people properly spaced for support." I said, "Then your real question is where are our people and how can we support you when you need us?" I got out a map, marked the positions of her stores, and showed her the support staff available. If I had answered her voiced question and nothing else, we never would have gotten to the real question. I had to find out her unvoiced question.
>
> Sometimes after I've answered a question, I'll ask, "Did I answer your question?" Many questions can be interpreted several ways. If you haven't given them the answer they expected, they may think you are avoiding them and assume the worst—that you don't want to answer. But if you ask whether you've answered their question, you have a second chance to answer the real question.

Dr. James Penton is also a firm believer in the importance of unasked questions: "Not all questions are verbal. Some are below the verbal level, actually subliminal. Being tuned in to *unstated* questions is extremely important! What is the real question? Salespeople should make sure they are answering the question the customer really wants to hear an answer to."

Are You an Expert?

I learned the importance of expertise from my son Tom, a talented chef. One day I was watching him make melon balls. A quick twist of the wrist with a tiny scoop and perfect spheres of melon piled up in a bowl. It looked so easy that I decided to try it. Soon oddly-shaped lumps of melon were flying behind the refrigerator, under the table, and down my shirt. My son tried to encourage me: "Just a few more weeks, Dad, and you'll be an expert too." I realized that to do anything well takes practice, commitment, and persistence.

Are You Persistent?

Once, super-salesperson Douglas E. Elwood absolutely couldn't arrange to meet with a prospect. The man was always in meetings or out of town. Doug learned that the man liked to jog early in the morning. The next time Doug was able to get through to him, he asked, "What are you doing at 5:00 A.M.?" At sunup Doug was waiting when the man returned from his run. Doug handed him some towels and brought out two thermoses: "Would you prefer orange juice or coffee?"

"You really want to sell me, don't you?"

"Partner, I didn't come out at five o'clock in the morning not to." Doug made a $100,000 sale.

Wynn Gilligan is another salesperson who refused to give up. She met a man at a party who became quite excited when he learned she sold cellular telephones. He asked her to call him at his office in a few days. When she did, he was too busy to talk and asked her to contact him later. This went on for *weeks!* "I started wondering if this could be the same eager prospect I met at the party," says Wynn. Each time he put her off, she'd ask, "When should I call again?" And then she would.

Finally, after four weeks of steady calling, she was able to meet with him. He told her that he already had prices on numerous phone systems and several were less expensive than hers. However, he was going to buy from her because he knew she'd be sure he got good service. Her persistence had proven that.

There is a post-script to this persistence story. The man's deposit check bounced. A lot of salespeople would have given up at this point. Not Wynn. "I called the man back and told him his bank said his check was no good." Fortunately it turned out to be a bank error and the bank wrote a letter of apology. Was a $1,000 sale worth all this effort? "I felt like giving up a dozen times, but I'm glad I didn't. You never know what will lead to something. Since then I've gotten a number of lucrative referrals from this one sale."

Are You Dedicated?

Sometimes the questions you ask yourself are the most productive. Lamyle Porter is co-owner of Broker One Mortgage Company, an investment intermediary that matches private investors with people needing mortgages and business loans. One day he telephoned the manager of a pension fund. "I won't buy anything," the manager said, "but if you want to stop by at 3 o'clock, I'll talk to you for five minutes."

Lamyle reached the lobby of the office building several minutes early and found that a power failure had knocked out all the elevators. His appointment was on the fifteenth floor. Now, here's where Lamyle asked the big question: *"What should I do now?"* This was, after all, a cold call, just a drop-in. The lobby was full of people waiting for pay phones to cancel appointments on the upper floors. Should he get in line? Or should he start climbing?

He climbed. And he made it on time. The astonished pension fund manager was impressed. "If you'll manage our money with this much commitment, I know you'll do a good job for us." The manager invested in two $250,000 loans on the spot. Lamyle secured a half million dollars by asking himself the right question. (That's close to $45,000 for each flight of stairs!)

Are You Willing to Be a Professional?

I have tried in this book to offer my ideas and examples to stimulate your own thinking. As a professional you will develop and hone your own repertoire of questions with your own unique style.

Each professional salesperson is like a great singer, dancer, or actor. The notes they sing, the steps they dance, or the lines they say may be the same ones that thousands have used before. Their greatness comes from their insight, their extra effort, and their sensitivity to the response of their buying audience. Each professional salesperson must combine the skills of a psychologist, a teacher, and a diplomat. Nothing worthwhile is easy. As Tarzan said, "It's a jungle out there." To succeed in sales, you must be willing to answer some hard questions.

Are you willing to be committed? Professional salespeople are committed to the selling profession. They'll stay for the long term results. They aren't put off or discouraged by temporary set backs.

Are you willing to expect? I'm absolutely certain that no one ever exceeds their own expectations. Professional salespeople have high expectations for themselves, their companies, their products and services, their customers, even their competition. How high are your standards? What do you expect of yourself?

Are you willing to have a high-faith factor? Do you believe that you either are or can become a high achiever in your chosen profession of sales? Have faith in your God-given talents, skills, and abilities.

Are you willing to develop your people skills? Do you know what makes people decide whether or not to do something? Have you discovered what motivates and closes the sale? There's an old saying: "The more personal, the more general." That means that most people feel the same way you feel deep inside. Most people want the same things you want.

Most people are motivated in the same ways you are motivated. Ask yourself what you feel, what you believe, what you value. Are you willing to develop and use that knowledge to understand others?

Are you willing to develop your product skills? There is no substitute for knowing your product inside and out. Professional salespeople read constantly, study informational audio and video tapes, and constantly ask questions to improve their understanding. They want to know everything they can about how their product works, how it can be used, and what it will do for their client. What is your program for learning more about your product?

Are you willing to study selling techniques? In addition to people and product knowledge, you must know the techniques of salesmanship. Selling is a game of fundamentals. Like golf, dancing, or body building, the more you learn about the technique, the more effective you will be in helping and serving your customer. What study program will you use to become a more effective salesperson?

Are you willing to try? It's not enough to have commitment, expectations, faith, knowledge, and desire. You've got to expend the effort and energy to grow as a professional salesperson. In all areas of your professional life you must try harder than you've ever tried before to improve yourself, to help your clients, to serve your customers. Years ago, when J. Paul Getty was the richest man in the world, he was asked how he became so wealthy. Getty replied, "I tried." "But," his questioner said, "*I* tried. I tried very hard." Getty said, "Yes, but I tried harder." How hard will you try?

Are you willing to care? You've heard the saying: "No one cares how much you know until they know how much you care." All professionals know they must have concern and care for their customers. They can't fake it. They must really want what is best for their clients more than they want the money they can earn from the sale. Can you be a truly caring professional?

Are you willing to go all the way? One salesman I know carries a 3"x 5"card in his pocket that says:

No hour is too early.
No hour is too late.
No distance is too far.
No amount is too small.

That philosophy is his commitment to go all the way for his customers. How early will you get up so you have extra time to study or to meet a client for breakfast? How late will you stay up to do record-keeping and planning? How far will you travel to call on a customer? How important is the small or occasional customer? Real professionals are willing to go all the way to be the success that they deserve to be.

Are you willing to expect, prepare, try, and care? That's what it takes to be a professional. If you're already a professional, you know who you are. If you're not there yet, take the advice of the director shoving the chorus girl on-stage in the old Hollywood musical: "You're going out a youngster, but you've got to come back a *star!*"

" My entire presentation is built on the 80/20 rule which I've taken in a different direction: I allow the prospect to talk 80 percent of the time while I ask questions 20 percent of the time to sort out the information. These questions can be as simple as, 'oh?' That means I want more information, 'Could you elaborate on that' or 'How do you mean that?' When I have an overwhelming urge to make a statement, I turn it into a question so I get a response."

Douglas E. Elwood
Speaker/Trainer

11

A Question a Day

*H*ere is a summary of selling questions to stimulate your own thinking. There are 365 of them, one for every day of the year. See if you can come up with a question of your own each day that will help you in some part of your presentation. Then try it out. Remember: A question a day can keep poverty away.

Motivation Questions

- How would you feel if . . . ?
- What do you think you need to get the job done?
- What do you feel is your biggest problem in . . . ?
- What's the most important thing about . . . ?
- What do you like most about . . . ?
- What do you like least about . . . ?
- What would *you* suggest?
- I understand that's how they feel, but what's your opinion?
- Why is that important to you?
- What do you think is a better way?
- Then how do you feel about . . . ?
- What would be your reaction to . . . ?
- Could you tell me more about that?
- Is quality control still your major concern?
- Are you still more concerned with growth than income from your investments?
- What is your competition doing?
- The last time we talked you were trying a new procedure. How is that working out for you?
- What would you like this to do for you?
- What's your biggest time pressure?
- Which of those options is more important to you right now?

- Are there any other ways this could help you?
- Is the immediate cost the most important factor in your decision, or are you more concerned with the long-term value?
- Are you concerned that this might not be the right step for you right now?
- How did you accomplish that?!
- What's the greatest need in your department right now?
- How are you planning to handle . . . ?
- How do you think that would affect . . . ?
- How long do you want to wait before you switch?
- If you could have this now, how would that affect . . . ?
- Would you prefer . . . ?
- What is the best thing about . . . ?
- What is the worst thing about . . . ?
- What motivates you?
- What is your goal?
- So what you mean by that is . . . ?

Prospecting Questions

- May I see the owner?
- I'm new to this area. Can you tell me whom I should talk to?
- If you were me and you could make only *one* more sales call, who would it be?
- Who's your toughest competitor? Could I use your name if I call on them?
- Is there someone else you think this service could really help?
- Would you give me a referral? Should I call or write first? Would you mind calling/writing to introduce me?
- What other new uses have you found for our product? What kind of people do you think could use it that way too?

Qualifying Questions

- What can I do to help you today?
- What do you think of this style?

- How does this model impress you?
- Is availability or delivery time important?
- Do you ever use . . . ?
- How long have you been with this company?
- Are you planning to add or lay off staff this year?
- What's your company's position in the market?
- How much could you write a check for right now? Not would, *could?*
- Is it too early to talk about financing?
- Have you made any preliminary arrangements about financing?
- How do you plan to finance this?
- What kind of payment plan . . . ?
- Who approves your purchase orders?
- How many of your employees are covered by your company's insurance plan?
- What do you plan to use a copy machine for?
- How do you arrange your executive travel?
- How old is the car you're driving now?
- How often does your present model need repairs?
- What are your plans for using this system?
- Will you use it at every site or only at the corporate office?
- What is your time frame for setting up this system?
- What do you now do by hand and what do you do by computer?
- What do you expect to accomplish with this system?
- Does your department use computers? No? Good, because . . . .
- Are you in charge of this department? No? That's great because . . . .
- Is that an unchangeable policy with you? Yes? That's excellent because . . . .
- If I were a magician and could change *anything* in your company (or situation, schedule, operations, etc.), what would that one thing be?
- What's your priority?
- What one thing would you like *never* to have to bother about again?

- Who do you use for your messenger service when something must get there immediately? How reliable are they?
- How are you keeping up with technology? What advances do you think would help you?
- Who makes the final decision?
- Who's in charge of quality control?
- Will you be selecting the equipment or is that done by the committee?
- Separate checks?
- Can you think of any reason—aside from the price—that you shouldn't have this right now?
- We have a variety of payment plans. What were you thinking of?
- Would you prefer a lower startup price or do you want to spend a little more now so you're sure of years of trouble-free service?
- Which is better: a large down-payment with small monthly payments? Or a small down payment and larger monthly payments?
- Do you agree that . . . ?
- Your situation seems very similar to what happened to one of my other clients. Shall I tell you how we solved his problem?
- Can you think of any other supplier with a better reputation for quality and service?
- How would you feel about trying the plan I've recommended?
- May I see you on Thursday at 4:00 o'clock?

Probing Questions

- If the world were perfect, what would you want my product to do for you?
- What kind of employee turnover do you have? What does it cost you when you train someone and then lose them?
- When you say your budget is limited, how limited do you mean?
- What problems do you absolutely want to avoid?

- What results do you expect? What results do you hope for?
- Is this for a special application or for general use?
- Where will you be using this?
- Where is your head office? How many branches?
- Who are your big competitors?
- Have you got a clear profile of your prospective customers? Have you defined your niche in the market?
- How long have you been looking? What has taken so long?
- What would your life be like if . . . ?
- How do you get your daily deposits to the bank?
- Are you trying to grow?
- What have you done in the past?
- Where have you tried to reach customers? Why do you think this target audience is best? Have you considered reaching a younger or older audience?
- What trends do you see in your field? How do you think they are going to affect your business?
- So improving that is your major concern right now?
- What role do you think employee satisfaction plays in productivity?
- Which is more important to you right now—gross revenue or bottom-line profit?
- Is it important to save money on maintenance?
- What would you have to find before you'd consider changing vendors?
- What do you like best about your current system? Least?
- Based on your years of experience with this company, what do you . . . ?
- As the new guy around here, you have a fresh perspective, so how do you . . . ?
- Do you feel that customer satisfaction increases profits?
- Could you give me an example of what you mean by more productivity? How would you measure it?
- What would represent success to you?
- Is down-time a problem for you? How do you handle it?
- Could you think of a better way to deal with that?
- Could I ask you a few more questions about that?

- Will ten work stations be enough for this department?
- What role will your higher-ups have in deciding? How many people will participate in the final decision?
- When you had this done the last time, what did they charge you?
- What do you hope will happen with this?
- Why are you automating?
- What kind of results are you looking for?
- Was it difficult for you to get the process rolling?
- What do you think is going to happen next?
- What's the worst thing you think might happen?
- Who have you been talking to and what have they been telling you about using this process?
- What have you heard about our company?
- Who will make the final decision?
- Who has the money?
- Is the project funded?
- When is the money available?
- What so you think this is going to do for your company?
- How are your August sales normally?
- Why do you think that was?
- Does your firm do a lot of business in that area?
- How would you use this feature?
- Can your organization help us get the information we need to come to a conclusion that we both agree with? Who can help us get this done?
- Do you think that employee turnover is too high for this department?
- You seem to have a lot of returns. Do you see quality control as a problem?
- How much do you use now? What do you anticipate you will need for the next year?
- What is your cost per _____?
- Do you ever run into problems because . . . ?
- How long does that take?
- What kind of training would your people need to use this? Are there any hidden human costs involved here? How would you handle personnel issues?

- Are you satisfied with your present service?
- What does your current supplier do that we can't do better?
- What kind of service do you expect?
- Who will be using this, you or your partner?
- When will you need this information?
- Will you be using this copy machine just for your office files or will you be sending out copies to customers?
- Is this a decision you are going to make now or later? When?
- What would *you* suggest?
- I understand that's what they feel, but what's your opinion?
- Why is that important to you?
- What do you think is a better way?
- Could you tell me more about that?
- What's the next thing you'd do if you could?
- What changes would you want to see?
- Is quality control still your major concern?
- The last time we talked you were trying a new procedure. How is that working out for you?
- What are your needs right now?
- What do you really want to accomplish?
- What can I do specifically to help you reach your goals?
- Can we discuss my fees?
- What criteria will you use to decide?
- What does your product or service really do for your customer?
- What are the key concerns of your customer after the purchase?
- How can the customer get in trouble by buying your product or service?
- What could annoy your customer about your product or service?
- What are the short-term business and personal objectives of your customer? What are their long-term objectives?
- Is your customer concerned about the opinion of anyone else? If so, what are the priorities of these other people?
- How are your other locations doing?

Presentation Questions

- Have you ever wondered why . . . ?
- What would you do if . . . ?
- What kind of person/company uses this? What's your image of a user?
- How long have you had this equipment?
- Which model is your favorite?
- If you could buy two instead of one, which would the second one be?
- When can you give me an appointment?
- How do you see yourself using this?
- May I show you how this feature could work for you?
- Is this big enough for your needs?
- Would you like to use this for a free trial?
- This plan saved your competitor $10,000 in the first year. Would you like me to figure what *your* savings would be?
- What's the worst thing that could happen to you?
- How competitive does your company want to be?
- What other models have you looked at? How close did they come to satisfying your needs?
- Is this what you had in mind?
- Have you ever watched a company fail? Do you think it was because of poor management?
- How much money/time will this save you?
- Did last year's storms catch you unprepared? What kind of damage did you have? Are you ready for this year?

Objection Questions

- If you had a bad steak in a restaurant, would you stop eating steak?
- Which means more to you—my option A or their option B?
- You feel our price is too high? Can you be more specific? Are you clear on the cost breakout?
- You say you're getting a few returns. How do you handle them?
- What made your new system so hard to learn?

- You say it's too complicated. Can you give me an example?
- Do you think your staff had a special reason for resisting the change?
- Are the employees/managers who objected to that still with your company?
- What affect has your new equipment had on your turn-over rate? Positive or negative? Why do you think that is?
- Is this equipment too sophisticated for your available work force? Are employee incentives to learn a new system too low? Are other working conditions at fault? Are there issues unrelated to the system that have affected productivity or error rate?
- I'm sorry I didn't make that clear. Would you like to see me demonstrate that again?
- You're sharp to pick up on that! Usually that's absolutely correct, but with this feature. . . . Is that one of your priorities?
- I can see why you figure it that way, and lots of our current customers started out like that too. Would you like me to try to arrange for you to talk to one of our best customers who . . . ?
- That shows you're really on top of the budget in your department, so. . . . How would a benefit like that work with your current program?
- You raise a good point. How exactly would this program integrate with your present system? Is that what you need to know first?
- Does that seem like a lot of money? Maybe this won't turn out to be the right program for you. Shall we stop and figure the actual cost so we can see how much money these features are going to save you?
- Obviously you would not take time to think this over unless you were really interested. Shall we make a quick list? What points do you need to consider?
- You want to wait? What's going to happen between now and that date that will make a difference? What will be more advantageous then?

- So the only undecided issue is how you will resolve your contractual arrangement with your current supplier? When do you think you'll be able to talk to your legal department about that? Shall I check back with you on Thursday?
- You think that could be cleared up by March?
- If I could show you how this improvement would pay for itself within a year, would you want to get started next week?
- If we can arrange to delay payments until the end of the quarter, would you like to be up and running next week and pay for it as it pays for itself?
- If I could help you solve that one problem, would using our service be a good step for your business right now?
- You think it will cost more to install this new valve than it will save you? Can I show you some comparison figures?
- So the price is your only problem?
- If I show you how you could afford to have what we are offering, would that solve your problem?
- Is there something about this product or our company that is making you hesitate? Is it something about me personally?
- Is that the only reason? What other reasons would you have to . . . ?
- Why do you think your managers are opposed to doing it that way?
- Are you seeing something that's not up to your standards?
- Is that the only thing holding you back?
- There's no way you'd reconsider this option . . . or is there?
- So you've absolutely decided against our product? What factors made up your mind?

Closing
- What is our next step?
- What do we need to do to get this thing done?
- What kind of support service do you want to have from us?
- Who else should I talk to before your company decides?

- Shall I check the delivery schedule on that?
- What is making you hesitate?
- How does that sound to you?
- What haven't I covered to your satisfaction?
- Is your home office going to have any problem with this?
- Can you think of any other solution that would work better for you?
- In your opinion, is this the best one for your Boston plant?
- How are your people going to feel about the changes these new terminals will produce?
- What's your gut reaction to replacing this unit instead of trying to keep it repaired?
- Should I put a hold on those for you?
- Will three be enough for the time being?
- What delivery date is good for you?
- How long would you like the warranty to run?
- Would you like our people to install that for you?
- Which payment plan would work best for you? So that's the one you want to implement? What date do you want to make the first installment?
- Would you like to schedule your people for our full-support training program *before* or *after* installation of the new equipment?
- Would you like six now and we'll hold the other six for delivery until you need them? Or would you rather have us send all twelve together?
- Would you like to order another gross and get the quantity discount?
- Check or charge?
- UPS or Express Mail?
- Do you want to handle the paperwork or shall I?
- Do you want to pick that up or shall we deliver it?
- Do you want us to load it in your car?
- Would you prefer a service contract or an extended warranty?
- Do you need to get a purchase order or is your signature sufficient?

- You have a lot of experience in this area. How would you get company approval for this purchase?
- Would you check this list and see if it covers all your immediate needs?
- Shall we walk this over to Purchasing for a signature so we can set up immediate delivery?
- Would your foreman like a chance to check this out today? How about taking the model down to your shop right now and I'll have the rest delivered next week?
- Do you want to get our 5% discount by ordering one more?
- Do you want to save on shipping by ordering an extra one now?
- Do you like this color? It's been discontinued and we've only got these left.
- Would you like to buy a case and get the twelfth can free?
- Can I show you a shirt and tie to go with your new suit?
- If you could choose a second one free, which would it be?
- Would you like to save 15% by booking before July 1st?
- Do you want to stock up? The price goes up on Sunday.
- Besides the turn-around time, what else would keep you from using our service?
- If it weren't for the high maintenance on this model, would it be perfect for your application?
- Setting cost aside, are there any features you need that this doesn't have? Except for money, what would stop you from going ahead?
- What is standing in the way of our doing business now? Is there anything that I can do that would get you to say 'yes'?
- What more can I do to make sure you are happy with this purchase?
- I agree to have half the units delivered by the first of the month, right? The rest will come two weeks later, right? And you agree that the signed contracts and the 10% down payment check for $10,000 will be at my office by Friday at 5:00, right?

Follow-Up Questions

- How did last Thursday's spots pull in Brooklyn?
- How are you doing with the new system?
- How is everything going with the new service?
- Was your delivery on time?
- Is it performing the way you expected?
- How would you rate our service? Is everything going okay?
- Are your people having any problems?
- What kind of speed/quantity time saving are you getting now? Do you have any hard figures? Is that what you hoped for?
- How are your people responding to the new system? Is this reaction you expected? What other feedback have you had?
- Is your current arrangement still giving you trouble? I've just gotten something that I think might solve your problem. Shall I come by tomorrow so you can take a look at it? Or would you like me to send the specs over?
- How is your new system interfacing with your old equipment? Do you see any problems down the road?
- Who else is going to be using this? What's the best way for me to interact with them?
- Have you found new needs as you've used it?
- Has increased production created new needs in your department? How can we help you to meet these new requirements?
- Have you found new ways to use our product? What new kinds of applications do you think we should consider?
- Who else do you think could use this?
- Was it a good decision?
- Does it do what we thought it would?
- Are you happy?
- Are you running low on any supplies?
- Is this a good time to rethink your system? You talked about it several months ago and I've got some suggestions for you if you're ready . . . ?

- I hear you called our customer service department with a problem . . . ?
- What kind of service did you get from our repair department? Is there any way you think this could be improved? Should I talk directly to the person who had the problem to see if I can help?
- What additional supports do you need from us?
- I know we're just one of your suppliers. How do you think we compare?
- What can I do to get you to purchase your next system from me?
- Where do we go from here?

I had six honest serving men
Who taught me all they knew.
There names were Where and What and
When
And Why and How and Who.

Rudyard Kipling

Index

About the Author

Bill Bethel is a nationally recognized, award winning speaker and sales consultant, with over 3000 speeches and seminars to his credit. He has been contributing to the bottom line of his clients and receiving rave reviews for their improved performance for over 30 years. He has trained and inspired thousands of sales people to achieve their share of "the American dream".

For information on speeches, seminars and sales training materials contact:

Bethel Leadership Institute
1376 Vancouver Ave.
Burlingame, California 94010
1-800-548-8001

Your Keys to Sales Success

❶ Idea-A-Day Guide to Super Selling and Customer Service

<u>Fifteen minutes a day</u> is all you'll need to ensure sales success all year long. The *Idea-a-Day Guide* is loaded with sales success ideas — 250 of them — one for each working day of the year. Not just another how-to book, *Idea-a-Day*'s unique organization gives you a new money-making idea on every page to give you a one-of-a-kind, hands-on reference you'll use every day of the year.

Paperback, 8 1/2" x 11," 15 Sections, 250 Forms
Checklist, Worksheets $19.95

❷ Implementing Sales Automation
by Paul H. Selden

This innovative guide takes you step-by-step through the minefield of sales force automation. You'll learn how to establish criteria for making your decision to automate, how to select hardware, how to select software, how to provide user support, how to measure results, and how to integrate your new system into all of your operations.
330-Page Text, 3-Ring Binder $139.00

❸ Cracking New Accounts *by Terry Booton*

New accounts are the lifeblood of every business. Terry Booton, the sales pro who teaches IBM's salespeople, shows you how to find potential new accounts, determine their needs, and win them for your company. The handy "making the sale" exam will show you the difference between real and apparent objections, how to qualify prospects, how to turn prospects into customers, and how to avoid self-sabotage.
235-Page Text; Hardcover $32.95

▼ ✂ & ✉

❹ Performance-Driven Sales Management

Step-by-step, you'll learn how to manage your sales force profitably. The 262-page manual updates the classic MBO (Management By Objectives) approach, concentrates on profitable applications and shows you how to instill the spirit of MBO throughout your sales force. An 80-page workshop is also included with case studies which enable you to apply the principles in real day-to-day situations.

262-Page Text, 60 Illustrations
80-Page Advertising Workshop
8 1/2" x 11" 3-Ring Binder $91.50

❺ Successful Sales Meetings: How to Plan, Conduct, and Make Meetings Pay Off

This step-by-step, how-to sales manager's guide will help you plan, run, and evaluate results-producing sales meetings every time. From defining objectives to evaluating results, this book's many checklists and planning forms will make your job simple and productive.

247 Pages, 8 1/2" x 11" 3-Ring Binder $91.50

❻ Complete Guide to Successful Sales Territory Planning & Management

Plan and manage:

- Your Profitability
- Your Markets
- Your Customers
- Your Products

Identify key accounts faster, set clearer objectives, measure results better, coach your team better. Plus the 130-page workshop helps you test and tract your skills and development with real-world problems and solutions.

220-Page Text
130-Page Sales Management Workshop
8 1/2" x 11" 3-Ring Binder $91.50

- -

Clip & Mail Order Form to: The Dartnell Corporation
4660 N. Ravenswood
Chicago, IL 60640

☎

FOR FASTER SERVICE CALL: U.S.: 1-800-621-5463
FAX: 312-561-3801
CANADA: 1-800-441-7878